The
ROAD
TO
SOCIALISM
AND THE
NEW WORLD ORDER

The Fabian Socialists' window, ordered by George Bernard Shaw in 1910.

Printed in the United States of America

ISBN 1-933641-10-X

The
ROAD
TO
SOCIALISM
AND THE
NEW WORLD ORDER

Dennis L. Cuddy, Ph.D.

"Fifty years is ample time in which to change a world and its people almost beyond recognition. All that is required for the task are a sound knowledge of social engineering, a clear sign of the intended goal—and power."

—Arthur C. Clarke, *Childehood's End* (1953)

"It is the system of nationalist individualism that has to go. . . . We are living in the end of the sovereign states. . . . In the great struggle to evoke a Westernized World Socialism, contemporary governments may vanish. . . . Countless people . . . will hate the new world order . . . and will die protesting against it."

—H. G. Wells, *The New World Order* (1393)

Socialist Party president candidate Norman Thomas in an interview during his 1948 presidential campaign revealed that "the American people will never knowingly adopt Socialism, but under the name of Liberalism they will adopt every fragment of the Socialist program until one day America will be a Socialist nation without knowing how it happened." This concept was expanded by his successor Michael Harrington in his books such as *Toward a Democratic Left* and *The Twilight of Capitalism*. And in the *Pittsburgh Press* (June 19, 1966), former head of the Communist Party of the USA, Earl Browder, is quoted as saying: "As time passes, the contrast between capitalist and socialist systems is blurred and the two giants of world power resemble one another more. . . . Americca is getting socialism on the installment plan through the programs of the welfare state. There is more real socialism in the United States today than there is in the Soviet Union. Americans may not be willing to vote for a program under the name of 'socialism' but put it under another label—whether liberal Republican or Democrat—and they're by and large in favor of the idea. . . . We have a large and growing degree of what 50 years ago would have been recognized as socialism. . . . Today the United States enjoys the socialism of the rich."

"Some even believe we [the Rockefeller family] are part of a secret cabal working against the best interests of the United States, characterizing my family and me as "internationalists" and of conspiring with others around the world to build a more integrated global political and economic structure—one world, if you will. If that's the charge, I stand guilty, and I am proud of it."

—David Rockefeller, *Memoirs* (2002)

Foreword

U.S. citizens find themselves in the unusual position of becoming dispossessed of constitutional freedoms in a silent, undeclared war. However, few know of the coercive nature or true power and influence of this socialist political monopoly. Fewer still comprehend the true side which some of the players occupy in this war. Many see the congressional "conservative" victories as a solution, without understanding that some of the top Republican leadership are internationalists, pushing the last pieces of the new world order in place.

Dr. Cuddy comes to the task of exposing the socialist movement well prepared by intellect, training, and opportunities, having been a senior associate at the U.S. Department of Education, one of the major transmission belts of world socialism. From this unique vantage point, he has a clear grasp of how the U.S. Department of Education as well as other agencies are being used to merge a once free people into the enslavement of world socialism. His training in political science, along with his in-depth research, give him a keen understanding of the political and spiritual players in this war. It is a mechanism designed to rob the U.S. of its high standard of living, and gradually to erode and eliminate religious freedom and political self-government.

I believe Dr. Cuddy has done a great service for his fellow Americans in exposing international socialism's plan. Widespread knowledge of the mechanisms used, as well as the people involved, can save future generations much heartache, if the current generation acts as bravely and decisively as their forefathers. The time is short and the stakes are high. Widespread distribution of this book can help to turn the tide.

—Shirley Correll, Ph.D.

Introduction

In looking at the movement toward a new world order based upon socialism, things historically are not always as they seem. For example, in Morris Hadley's book, *Arthur Twining Hadley* (1948), about his own father (a member of Skull & Bones), he revealed: "Theodore Roosevelt would term Arthur Hadley his fellow anarchist and say that if their true views were known they would be so misunderstood that they both would lose their jobs as president of the United States [Roosevelt] and president of Yale University [Hadley]."

And Col. Elisha Garrison in *Roosevelt, Wilson and the Federal Reserve Law* (1931) wrote about "people who hoped and half believed that Theodore Roosevelt might end by becoming America's great Socialist leader."

That the movement would proceed gradually came a few years later, as Socialist Party presidential candidate Norman Thomas revealed that "the American people will never knowingly adopt Socialism, but under the name of Liberalism they will adopt every fragment of the Socialist program until one day America will be a Socialist nation without knowing how it happened."

The gradual pursuit of world domination was Cecil Rhodes' (as well as the Fabian socialists') plan (including Rhodes Scholars like Bill Clinton) to be carried out by his "secret society" formed February 5, 1891. Five years later, Gaetano Mosca in *The Ruling Class: Elementi Di Scienza Politica* (1896) described the need for the "circulation of elites" from below (such as Rhodes' "Association of Helpers"), so that avenues toward obtaining elite status would not be prohibited by purely hereditary membership. Christopher Hitchens, the self-described socialist friend of Bill Clinton, who was at Oxford University when Clinton was a Rhodes Scholar there, said on C-Span, August 23, 1993, that "it is, of course, the case that there is a ruling class in this country, and that it has allies internationally." Ten years after Mosca's book,

Vilfredo Pareto wrote *The Mind and Society* (1906), in which he conceded that the governing elite "must now and again bend the knee to the whims of the ignorant and domineering sovereigns or parliaments, but they are soon back at their tenacious, patient, never-ending work, which is of much the greater consequence."

Both Mosca's and Pareto's theories are further explained in *The Theory of Democratic Elitism: A Critique* (1967) by Peter Bachrach, who "thanks the Rockefeller Foundation for its generous grant, without which the essay could not have been written."

One of "The Group" helping to carry out Rhodes' plan was P. E. Corbett, who in 1942 authored *Post-War Worlds* stating: "It must be recognized that the law of nations takes precedence over national law.... A world association binding together and coordinating regional groupings of states may evolve toward one universal federal government."

Think of this in terms of NAFTA and GATT's World Trade Organization paving the way in the future for a world socialist government. Corbett continued:

> The process will have to be assisted by the deletion of the nationalistic material employed in educational textbooks.... World government is the ultimate aim, but there is more chance of attaining it by gradual development.... Men ... are looking to ... common economic agencies for advice and control.... An Economic and Financial Organization, embracing Trade, Development, and Migration Commissions, and a Central Bank. The functions of these institutions would be to regulate the production and distribution of raw materials and food, control the flow of inter-regional investment and migration, etc.

The global elite's plan is to synthesize western capitalism and eastern communism into a world socialist government. Their model experiment for this began in July 1997 when Hong Kong (capitalist) was turned over to China (communist), resulting in Hong Kong's synthesis into a socialist government.

Shortly after the Second World War, the United World Federalists were formed with Cord Meyer as president, partly due to the urging of W. T. Holiday, president of Standard Oil of Ohio. Standard Oil had been associated with the Rockefellers for some time, and in 1973 David Rockefeller established the Trilateral Commission with Zbigniew Brzezinski as its first director. David Rockefeller would be chairman of the Council on Foreign Relations from 1970 to 1985, and Brzezinski would be a member of the CFR and President Jimmy Carter's National Security Advisor.

Carter appointed CFR member and Trilateralist Richard Gardner (who was a member of the Consultative Planning Group for the 1976 Declaration of Interdependence) as his ambassador to Italy after Gardner authored his infamous article "The Hard Road to World Order" in the CFR's *Foreign Affairs* (April 1974). Many people are familiar with his statement in this article that "the 'house of world order' will have to be built from the bottom up rather than from the top down, . . . but an end run around national sovereignty, eroding it piece by piece, will accomplish much more than the old-fashioned frontal assault."

However, most people aren't aware of how the "end run around national sovereignty" would occur. When you, the reader, reflect upon the recent heated debate over the General Agreement on Tariffs and Trade (GATT) and the World Trade Organization (WTO), during which Senator Robert Dole said about GATT and the WTO that "the sovereignty issue is a red-herring, and this is not about a New World Order" (and Rush Limbaugh refused to run ads by Phyllis Schlafly and Pat Buchanan against GATT and the WTO), just remember what Gardner also said in his 1974 article:

> The hopeful aspect of the present situation is that even as nations resist appeals for "world government" and "the surrender of sovereignty," technological, economic and political interests are forcing them to establish more and more far-reaching arrangements to manage their mutual interdependence. . . . Among other things, we will be seeking new rules in the GATT to cover a whole range of hitherto unregulated nontariff barriers. These will subject countries to an unprecedented degree of international surveillance over up to now sacrosanct "domestic" policies. . . . GATT arrangements for consultation, conciliation and enforcement of its decisions will have to be greatly improved. . . . Despite the constitutional impasse over U.N. *peacekeeping,* there will in practice be increasing resort to U.N. forces to contain local conflicts. . . . New GATT procedures should be created requiring advance notice, consultation, authoritative interpretation of the rules, and settlement of disputes by impartial conciliation commissions under GATT auspices.

... Multilateral sanctions may even have to be applied to countries that are not GATT members ...

(worth remembering regarding GATT and WTO proponents' claim that the U.S. can simply withdraw from them if things don't go our way). Gardner continued:

> Unilateral U.S. action will look to others as a destructive act of nationalism unless it is related to multilateral rules and procedures.... Some mutually agreed limitations of sovereignty are essential to give full possibilities to the sovereignty of all.... We will need to find better ways of enforcing the rules, as by multilateral action that denies benefits and applies punishments.... We might begin, very gradually, to deflect the divisive tendencies of nationalism that are now emerging and to exploit the latent possibilities for strengthening the international system.

During Bill Clinton's 1992 presidential campaign, Gardner (a Rhodes Scholar like Bill Clinton) advised him on foreign affairs, and President Clinton named Gardner as ambassador to Spain. Strobe Talbott (Rhodes Scholar roommate of Bill Clinton at Oxford University, CFR director, and Trilateralist) would be named by President Clinton as Number 2 at the State Department, and he would be given the first "Norman Cousins Global Governance Award" by the World Federalist Association for his *Time* (July 20, 1992) article "The Birth of the Global Nation," in which he declared that "perhaps national sovereignty wasn't such a great idea after all.... But it has taken the events in our own wondrous and terrible century to clinch the case for world government."

President Clinton wrote a letter on White House stationery on June 22, 1993, to the World Federalist Association congratulating Talbott on receiving the award, and stating: "Norman Cousins worked for world peace and world government. ... Best Wishes for an enjoyable reception and for future success."

The World Federalist Association (successor to United World Federalists mentioned earlier, and now called Citizens for Global Solutions) is probably the leading organization today working for world federal government, and for President Clinton to acknowledge Norman Cousins' (previous WFA president) work specifically for "world government" and to wish the WFA "future success" says it all! In 1995 the WFA published *The Genius of Federation: Why World Federation Is the Answer to Global Problems,* in which was described a step-by-step advancement toward global governance:

> Let the U.N. establish new agencies such as an International Criminal Court (which can try individuals for violations of international law) or a U.N. Arms Control and Disarmament Agency.... By means of these voluntarily funded functional agencies, national sovereignty would be gradually eroded until it is no longer an issue. Eventually a world federation can be formally adopted with little resistance.

How this was to fit with the "New Age" was explained many years ago by occultist Alice Bailey (whose works were originally published by Lucifer Publishing Co.) in *The Rays and the Initiations* (published in 1960, after her death in 1949), in which she described "the Aryan race," a "point of light," a "new vision," and the "Lord of the World" with the "new world religion" in "the coming New Age" based upon synthesis. She explained:

> Synthesis dictates the trend of all the evolutionary processes today; all is working towards larger unified blocs, towards amalgamations, international relationships, global planning, brotherhood, economic fusion, the free flow of commodities everywhere, interdependence, fellowship of faiths ... (one result of this synthesis energy has been the forming of the United Nations).... Seventh ray energy is the energy needed to bring order out of chaos and rhythm to replace disorder. It is this energy which will bring in the new world order for which all men wait. ... Nothing can arrest this activity; all that is happening today as men search for the new ways, for organized unity and peaceful security.... The white magic of right human relations cannot be stopped.... The lord of the Ray is cooperating with the Lord of the World to bring about the needed "re-forming."

(See quotes from Robert Hugh Benson's 1907 book *Lord of the World* on page 127 of my book here.)

The Road to Socialism
and the New World Order

So'cial-ism (so'shal.izm). N, A political and economic theory of social organization based on collective or governmental ownership and democratic management of the essential means for the production and distribution of goods; ... Socialism aims to replace competition by co-operation and profit seeking by social service, and to distribute income and social opportunity more equitably than they are now believed to be distributed.

— *Webster's New International Dictionary*

Socialism (1839). A theory or policy of social organization which advocates the ownership and control of the means of production, capital, land, property, etc. by the community as a whole, and their administration or distribution in the interest of all.

— *Shorter Oxford English Dictionary,* 1970, Great Britain

Many today are looking for a "conspiracy" behind the movement for world government, but they may not find it in the usual sense of a secret cabal meeting clandestinely. Rather, what is occurring is a type of "networking" of like-minded individuals as described in Marilyn Ferguson's *The Aquarian Conspiracy* (1980). For years, leaders in education, industry, the media, banking, etc., have promoted those with the same world view as theirs. Of course, someone might say that just because individuals promote their friends doesn't constitute a conspiracy, and that's true in the usual sense. However, it does represent an "open conspiracy" as described by noted Fabian socialist H. G. Wells in *The Open Conspiracy: Blue Prints for a World Revolution* (1928). Among those congratulating Wells on this book were Carl Jung in a letter June 11, 1928 (and who later that year wrote "your ideas are such im-

Dr. med. C. G. Jung LL. D.   *228 Seestrasse*
                                                Küsnacht-Zürich

                                                June 11th 1928

            My dear Mr. Wells:

                        I thank You for sending me your very
interesting and suggestive book "The open Conspiracy", and I marvel
that your interest is still going out to this fiction of a world that
apparently wants to be improved. They are at this job since two thousand years and it is still doubtful wether they have succeeded or not.
Well, let us try anyhow!

            I am going to send you my new English publication as soon as it
is out.

            Very sincerely yours

                        C. G. Jung.

portant a message to the world"), Bertrand Russell in a letter May 24, 1928, saying "I do not know of anything with which I agree more entirely. . . . Among younger men, I believe your support would be very meagre. . . . Haldane would not forego the pleasure to be derived from the next war," and President Woodrow Wilson's chief advisor, Col. Edward M. House, in a letter November 4, 1928 saying he was "reading it with care, with pleasure and with profit. The world indeed is in flux, and just what the outcome may be lies on the knees of the gods. In the adjustment of things this book should wield a profound influence, for no man in all the world has a wider audience than you."

For decades, the power elite have made a conscious effort to get key people with their same world view into key positions of influence. This is what the Educational Trust (founded in 1915) did. James McKeen Cattell (Deweyite educator) wrote in the November 1923 *Annals of the American Academy of Political and Social Science* that one of the purposes of The Psychological Corporation (founded in 1921) was:

104 East 68th Street,
New York City.
Nov. 4. 1928.

EDWARD M HOUSE,
AUSTIN TEXAS

Dear Mr. Wells::

Upon our return to
New York I find <u>The Open Conspiracy</u>
sent by the publishers with your
compliments.

I greatly appreciate your
thinking of me and am reading it
with care, with pleasure and with
profit.

The world indeed is in flux,
and just what the outcome may be
lies on the knees of the gods. In
the adjustment of things this book
should wield a profound influence,
for no man in all the world has a
wider audience than you.

With all good wishes,

Sincerely yours,

H. G. Wells Esq.
Easton Glebe,
Dunmow, Essex.

To get the best kind of people and to put them in the situations in which they will behave in the way best for themselves and for others, is more fundamental than any other enterprise of society. It is necessary to organize means by which this work can be accomplished. . . . Psychology is concerned with the causes of conduct and its control.

And today, Council on Foreign Relations (CFR) president Leslie Gelb said on "The Charlie Rose Show" (May 4, 1993) that "you [Charlie Rose] had me on [before] to talk about the new world order. . . . I talk about it all the time. . . . It's one world now. . . . The Council [CFR] can find, nurture, and begin to put people in the kinds of jobs this country needs. And that's going to be one of the major enterprises of the Council under me." Previous CFR chairman (1953–70) John J. McCloy actually said they have been doing this since the 1940s (and before). This was also the purpose of Cecil Rhodes' secret "Society of the Elect."

The first notable to specifically call for "world government" was Dante in *De Monarchia* in A.D. 1313 (and he emphasized points of light in *The Divine Comedy*). This was followed by Henry IV's "Great Design," which would be invoked by Abbe de Saint-Pierre Charles-Irenee Castel in *Le Projet de Paix Perpetuelle* (1713) proposing an international organization (with a permanent arbitration council) to secure universal peace. After the "Great Design," there were various utopian planned socialist societies proposed, such as the one described in *New Atlantis* (published posthumously, 1627) by Sir Francis Bacon, alleged author of Shakespeare's works (Bacon considered himself a biblical scholar, and *Macbeth,* Act 4, Scene 1, line 10, states, "Double, double toil and trouble; fire burn and cauldron bubble," while Revelations 18:6,8 contains, ". . . double unto her double according to her works: in the cup which she hath filled fill to her double . . . and she shall be utterly burned with fire . . .").

But it was not until the early 1800s that the movement toward world socialist government began in earnest with the Comte de Saint-Simon. In 1803 he stated his goal as the "universal association" of all men in "all spheres of their relationships." He advocated a type of industrial feudalism (his ancestor, Charlemagne, had initiated feudalism) ruled by a self-appointed elite, who would be socialist (Pierre Leroux actually coined the word "socialism") and "scientific" in nature. Saint-Simon's "science" would be called "sociology." This term was actually coined around 1838 by Saint-Simon's 1818–1824 secretary, Auguste Comte, who developed the "Religion of Humanity." According to author Erica Carle, integrity and character were unimportant in the World Management System proposed by Comte, who wrote in his *System of Positive Polity* (vol. 2, 1851, p. 327): "When the system is fully regulated, the effect of this will be to secure greater unity, by diminishing the influence of personal character." (This seems relevant because in the late twentieth century a large number of Americans believed President Clinton's personal character didn't matter.)

Saint-Simon's "social science" (Comte's "sociology") would also serve as the basis for a socialistic system developed by Fourier at about the same time. Ludwig von Westphalen taught the collectivist socialism of Saint-Simon to his son-in-law, Karl Marx, who also studied Fourier and used Proudhon's term, "scientific socialism." Marx's dialectics (thesis and antithesis forming a synthesis) were developed from Hegel, who had succeeded Fichte (who also influenced Marx) at the University of Berlin in 1814 and who believed that the collectivist-socialist state was all, or practically all. In *The Impact of Science on Society* (1953), Bertrand Russell will state that "Fichte laid it down that education should aim at destroying free will, so that, after pupils have left school, they should be incapable, throughout the rest of their lives, of thinking and acting otherwise than as their schoolmasters would have wished."

The conspiratorial nature of Marx's efforts perhaps originated with the League of the Just, which came from the Parisian Outlaws League (possibly including members of Adam Weishaupt's dispersed Illuminati who influenced the French Revolution). Picking up from Babeuf's "Conspiracy of Equals" during the French Revolution, Buonarroti in the early 1800s formed conspiratorial secret societies in order gradually to erode societies and form "a new social order." In his book *Conspiracy for Equality,* his "order" of elitists would nationalize most of the wealth of countries and the family unit would be undermined, with "the country taking possession of every individual at birth and never quitting him until death."

In modifying human behavior to accept this socialism, he indicated activities in certain areas should be "voluntary and unconstrained" but really meant "compulsory" and "coerced." Today in the U.S. there are efforts to nationalize key aspects of life, such as police, health plans, and education standards. And "voluntary" service is often "coerced" in the form of "requirements" for graduation, college admission, employment, and job promotion.

Buonarroti wrote that his "plan" for the "order" was that it would "extend itself without being noticed everywhere in order ... to cover the globe; it has already spread roots over a vast surface." Karl Marx and Friedrich Engels contemplated publishing a German edition of this book, and in the late 1800s Engels wrote *The Origin of the Family,* in which he stated:

> ... the first condition for the liberation of the wife is to bring the whole female sex back into public industry, and this in turn demands the abolition of the monogamous family as the economic unit of society. ... With the transfer of the means of production into common ownership, the single family ceases to be the economic unit of society. Private housekeeping is transformed into a social industry. The care and education of the children becomes a public affair; society looks after all children alike, whether they are legitimate or not. This removes all anxiety about the "consequences," which today is the most essential social—moral as well as economic—factor that prevents a girl from giving herself completely to the man she loves. Will not that suffice to bring about the gradual growth of unconstrained sexual intercourse and with it a more tolerant public opinion in regard to a maiden's honor and a woman's shame?

Does this type of "free love" promiscuity sound familiar?

Five years after Marx's *Communist Manifesto* (1848), socialist John Ruskin (on his grave is the swastika, which would also be the symbol of the Thule Society to which Hitler would belong) wrote *Stones of Venice* (1853), in which he declared: "Education is the leading of human souls to what is best and making what is best out of them. ... Education does not mean teaching people what they do not know. It means teaching them to behave as they do not behave."

Thus the state must change people's behavior to what it knows is best, and in *Time and Tide* (1867) Ruskin wrote that "the first duty of a State is to see that every child born therein shall be well housed, clothed, fed and educated. ... But in order to the effecting this the Government must have an authority over the people of which we now do not so much as dream."

One who would "dream" of how actually to accomplish this would be Ruskin disciple Cecil Rhodes, with his plan for world domination to be carried out by a secret society and through Rhodes scholarships (Bill Clinton would receive one). Bill Clinton's mentor at Georgetown University, Prof. Carroll Quigley, would write from the "secret records" of the world planners in *Tragedy and Hope* (1966) that Rhodes' plan would be carried forward in part by the Round Table Groups, and that in the U.S. a copy of their Oxford headquarters would be the Institute for Advanced Study (headed by Abraham Flexner of the Carnegie Foundation for the Advancement of Teaching, Rockefeller's General Education Board, and of the Education Trust founded in 1915 to direct the future of American Education) at Princeton University where Woodrow Wilson was president from 1902–1910. It is interesting to note that Prof. Quigley (whose tutor at Harvard University had been Rhodes Scholar Crane Brinton) died not too long after the March 23, 1975, *Washington Post* article about him titled "The Professor Who Knew Too Much." George Orwell died the year after *1984* was published. And coincidentally, President Lincoln was assassinated less than five months after he wrote to William Elkin (November 21, 1864):

> I see in the near future a crisis approaching that unnerves me and causes me to tremble for the safety of my country. As a result of the war, corporations have been enthroned and an era of corruption in high places will follow, and the money power of the country will endeavor to prolong its reign by working upon the prejudices of the people until all wealth is aggregated in a few hands, and the Republic is destroyed. I feel at this moment more anxiety for the safety of my country than ever before, even in the midst of war.

In 1861, President Lincoln had gone to New York to ask for loans to prosecute the war against the Confederacy. He rejected the bankers' offer of loans at 24–36 percent interest, and instead decided to have the government print its own "greenbacks" rather than go into debt. Almost $450 million of these new bills were printed during the war at no interest to the federal government. Then on April 14, 1865, Lincoln was assassinated by John Wilkes Booth, a member (along with Jesse James, a sixth cousin to James Garrison, former president of the Gorbachev Foundation/USA) of a secret society called Order of the Knights of the Golden Circle, which had ties to a French secret society (called The Seasons) that had been a branch of the Illuminati. The front page of the *Vancouver Sun* (May 2, 1934) carried a news article about Vancouver lawyer-economist Gerald McGeer testifying to a House of Commons (Canadian) committee that based upon his study of unexpurgated copies of evidence given by secret service agents at Booth's trial (after Booth's death), McGeer declared the only group that could benefit by Lincoln's death, and who had the money to carry out such a plan, was the international bankers' group. McGeer stated that

> Lincoln was wont to describe the men opposing his Greenback Currency policy as "the secret foes of the nation." ... There was only one group in the world at that time who could finance anything they cared to attempt without regard to cost. . . . They were the men interested in . . . the right of the bankers to manage the currency and credit of every nation in the world. . . .

Cecil Rhodes first developed his plan in *Confession of Faith* (1875), which he included in his first will (1877). And in this 1875 work, he stated: "The [Secret] Society should inspire and even own portions of the press, for the press owns the minds of the people."

Nine years later, the Fabian (socialist) Society began (1884, the year after Marx's death). In 1895, the Fabians began the London School of Economics (whose graduates would include President John F. Kennedy). The American counterpart of the Fabian Society would be the Intercollegiate Socialist Society (the name would change to League for Industrial Democracy in 1921, with John Dewey as president in 1939–40), and the American counterpart of the London School of Economics would be the New School for Social Research (founded in 1919).

In the Introduction to *The Great Deceit* (1964 Veritas Foundation study), Archibald Roosevelt (son of Theodore Roosevelt) stated: "Socialists have infiltrated our colleges, our schools, our law courts, our government, our media of communications and our churches."

The Veritas study went on to say that "the Fabian [gradualist] Socialist movement is made up of a relatively small number of people who have developed the technique of influencing large masses of people to a very high degree."

Roosevelt indicated that in nearly every school, there are frequent reports on children's "group cooperation" (socialism emphasizes the group over the individual). One of the "media of communications" that has been "influencing large masses of people" has been the *New York Times,* about which Herman Dinsmore (foreign editor of the *New York Times* from 1951–1960) wrote in his 1969 book, *All the News That Fits:* "The *New York Times* today is deliberately pitched to the so-called liberal point of view. . . . Positively and negatively, the weight of *The Times* has generally fallen on the side of the communists since the end of World War II."

In terms of controlling mankind, prominent sociologist Lester Ward wrote in *Dynamic Sociology or Applied Social Science* (1883): "All results are accomplished by FORCE. The so-called 'abstract RIGHTS' of mankind must be denied if society is ever to become the arbiter of its own destiny." And in 1901, the "father of American sociology," socialist Edward Alsworth Ross, wrote *Social Control* revealing that social checks and stimuli "are managed by a rather small knot of persons . . . the Elite. . . . Judgment may be moulded as well as the will and the feelings."

This was the same year in which the American Socialist Society was incorporated, and for the next five years, plans were developed for the Rand School of Social Science, founded in 1906. Two of "the Elite" managing affairs were John D. Rockefeller and J. P. Morgan and one of their prime areas of management was the press. In Ferdinand Lundberg's *America's 60 Families* (1937), one finds that

> the Senate Privileges and Elections Committee in 1912 unearthed a letter that Representative Joseph Sibley (PA), the [Rockefeller] Standard Oil pay-off man in Washington, had written in 1905 to John D. Archbold [Standard Oil's money provider]. Sibley said, "An efficient literary bureau is needed, not for a day or a crisis but a permanent healthy control of the Associated Press and kindred avenues. It will cost money but it will be the cheapest in the end." . . . C. S. Mellen of the [J.P. Morgan-controlled] New Haven Railroad admitted that more than one thousand New England Newspapers were on the New Haven payroll.

Many people wonder how capitalists like J. P. Morgan and John D. Rockefeller could be on such friendly terms with socialism, but one must remember that there is a difference between capitalism and monopoly capitalism. While socialism imposes more government regulations or controls than capitalism, monopoly capitalists can believe that through financial contributions they can persuade politicians to impose government regulations or controls favorable to the monopoly capitalists against potential competitors.

In the February 9, 1917, *Congressional Record,* Rep. Oscar Callaway (Texas) inserted the following statement:

> In March, 1915, the J. P. Morgan interests, the steel, shipbuilding, and powder interests, and their subsidiary organizations got together 12 men high up in the newspaper world and employed them to select the most influential newspapers in the United States and sufficient number of them to control generally the policy of the daily press of the United States. These 12 men worked the problem out by selecting 179 newspapers, and then began, by an elimination process, to retain only those necessary for the purpose of controlling the general policy of the daily press throughout the country. They found it was only necessary to purchase the control of 25 of the greatest papers. The 25 papers were agreed upon; emissaries were sent to purchase the policy, national and international, of these papers; an agreement was reached; the policy of the papers was bought, to be paid for by the month; an editor was furnished for each paper to properly supervise and edit information regarding the questions of preparedness, militarism, financial policies, and other things of national and international nature considered vital to the interests of the purchasers.

As stated above, not only was J. P. Morgan "managing" affairs, but so too was John D. Rockefeller (Standard Oil) as revealed by investigative reporter Thomas Lawson in "Frenzied Finance" (*Everybody's Magazine,* August 1904):

> There gather each day, between the hours of eleven and twelve o'clock, all the active men whose efforts make "Standard Oil" what "Standard Oil" is. . . . Reports are presented . . . republics and empires made and unmade. . . . The success of "Standard Oil" is largely due to two things—the loyalty of its members to each other and to "Standard Oil" and the punishment of its enemies. Each member before initiation knows its religion to be reward for friends and extermination of enemies. Once a man is within the magic circle . . . punishment for disloyalty is sure and terrible, and

in no corner of the earth can he escape it, nor can any power on earth protect him from it. . . . Every twist and turn in the pedigree and records of Republicans and Democrats are as familiar to [the head of Standard Oil] as the "dope sheets" are to the gambler, for is he not at the receiving end of the greatest information bureau in the world? A "Standard Oil" agent is in every hamlet in the country.

Robert Minor's cartoon depicting J. P. Morgan, Andrew Carnegie, John D. Rockefeller, Teddy Roosevelt, and other men of wealth welcoming Karl Marx's socialism (*St. Louis Post-Dispatch,* 1911).

Similarly, New York City mayor John Hylan would later state that

The real menace of our republic is this invisible government which like a giant octopus sprawls its slimy length over city, state and nation. Like the octopus of real life, it operates under cover of a self-created screen. It seizes in its long and power-ful tentacles our executive officers, our legislative bodies, our schools, our courts, our newspapers, and every agency created for the public protection. It squirms in the jaws of darkness and thus is the better able to clutch the reins of government, secure enactment of the legislation favorable to corrupt business, violate the law with impunity, smother the press and reach into the courts. To depart from mere generalizations, let me say that at the head of this octopus are the Rockefeller-Standard Oil interests and a small group of powerful banking houses generally referred to as the international bankers. The little coterie of powerful international bankers virtually run the United States government for their own selfish purposes. They practically control both parties, write political platforms, make catspaws of party leaders, use the leading men of private organizations, and resort to every device to place in nomination for high public office only such candidates as will be amenable to the dictates of corrupt big business. They connive at centralization of government on the theory that a small group of hand-picked, privately controlled individuals in power can be more easily handled than a larger group among whom there will most likely be men sincerely interested in public welfare. These international bankers and Rockefeller-Standard Oil interests control the majority of newspapers and magazines in this country. They use the columns of these papers to club into submission or drive out of office public officials who refuse to do the bidding of the powerful corrupt cliques which compose the invisible government. (See *New York Times,* March 27, 1922.)

Perhaps this is what President Woodrow Wilson (who had been a trustee of the Carnegie Foundation) was referring to when he wrote in *The New Freedom* (1913):

Since I entered politics, I have chiefly had men's views confided to me privately. Some of the biggest men in the U.S., in the field of commerce and manufacturing, are afraid of somebody, are afraid of something. They know that there is a power somewhere so organized, so subtle, so watchful, so interlocked, so complete, so pervasive, that they had better not speak above their breath when they speak in condemnation of it.

Mrs. J. P. Morgan's niece in 1906 married Frederick Keppel, who would become a confidential clerk in the War Department during World War I. He shared living quarters with Felix Frankfurter, and socialist-communist ACLU founder Roger Baldwin wrote that after Frankfurter and Walter Lippmann left their War Office jobs, "I have to depend entirely upon Keppel." In December 1922, Keppel was elected president of the Carnegie Corporation of New York.

That the Carnegie Foundation as well as the Rockefeller Foundation's General Education Board (Andrew Carnegie was a member) were receiving increasing scrutiny from Congress was evident from the following discussion in the January 26, 1917, *Congressional Record*. Regarding these two entities, Senator George Chamberlain (Oregon) described "activities that have been indulged in through the [U.S.] Bureau of Education by agencies which seem to me to be inimical to the education of the youth of this country."

He referred to "pets" of the bureau, like Prof. Charles Judd, who were paid one dollar per year by the bureau, and then Prof. Judd used the government's franking privilege through the bureau to spread his ideology. Other "pets" included "progressive" education placement barons like Ellwood Cubberley of Stanford University, Paul Hanus of Harvard University, and George Strayer of Columbia University Teachers College, who was a member of the Educational Trust and would say "Give 'em the axe" regarding disobedient subordinates, and who would become head of the National Education Association a couple of years later. Senator Chamberlain noted that Prof. Judd's view went out

> as though it were actually an authoritative publication of the views of the Government. . . . They are moving with military precision all along the line, to get control of the education of the children of the land. I venture to say that if you put the educational system of this country in the hands of any particular class of individuals, in two generations, they can practically change the form of our Government by educating the children along certain lines. . . . I do not think any particular set of individuals ought to have exclusive control of the education of children.

Senator Miles Poindexter (Washington) then said: "The cult of Rockefeller, the cult of Carnegie, in the viewpoint which they represent in political economy and in government, is just as much to be guarded against in the educational system of the country as a particular religious sect."

Senator William Kenyon (Iowa) next related that

> there are certain colleges in this country that have sought endowments, and the agent of the Rockefeller Foundation or the educational board had gone out and

examined the curriculum of these colleges and compelled certain changes to be made in the studies and the curriculum. It seems to me that it is one of the most dangerous things that can go on in a Republic to have an institution of this power apparently trying to shape and mold the thought of the young people of the country. ... Professors who did not teach along the line that they might decree had in some instances been compelled to give up their positions.

Senator John Works (California) then recalled "a bill introduced [in the Senate] providing for the incorporation of the Rockefeller Foundation, a new corporation, for educational purposes.... It simply shows the tendency on the part of these people who are attempting to get control of the whole educational work of the country."

Returning to Felix Frankfurter, Teddy Roosevelt on December 19, 1917, wrote a letter accusing him of "taking on behalf of the Administration an attitude which seems to me to be fundamentally that of Trotsky and the other Bolsheviki leaders in Russia; an attitude which may be fraught with mischief to this country."

That Roosevelt's prediction was correct was supported by Lt.-Col. J. B. Mac-Lean, who wrote "Why Did We Let Trotzky Go? Canada Lost an Opportunity to Shorten the War" in the Canadian magazine *MacLean's* (June 1919), in which he revealed:

Official reports . . . show that but for the Russian breakdown [revolution] the war would have been over a year earlier. . . . On March 26,1917, the night before Trotzky sailed [from New York], . . . [he] explained quite frankly and clearly that "they were going to Russia to push the Revolution as it ought to be pushed. You who stay here must work hand in hand with the Revolution in Russia, for only in that way can you accomplish revolution in the United States."

Lt.-Col. MacLean goes on to say that the British Secret Service had Trotzky detained at Halifax, Nova Scotia, but he was ordered released

at the request of the British Embassy at Washington over the head of the British and American Intelligence Department [which knew he was a German, not a Russian, and plentifully supplied with money from German sources in New York];

and that the Embassy acted on the request of the U.S. State Department, who was acting for someone else.

"Someone else" probably referred to President Wilson's chief adviser, Col. Edward M. House, who had informed his friend, Sir William Wiseman (chief of the British Secret Service in the U.S. during World War I, who after the war joined Kuhn, Loeb & Co. bankers), of President Wilson's desire that Trotsky be released. According to Arthur Willert (Washington correspondent for *The (London) Times* during the war, and friend of Wiseman) in his *The Road to Safety* (1952), early Russian Revolutionary leader Alexander Kerensky (a self-described "social democrat") had telegraphed President Wilson persuading him to intervene on behalf of Trotsky. Wiseman, who initially warned the Canadians about Trotsky's arrival, forwarded Wilson's request to London and Trotsky was released. This was good news to German military intelligence, which was at about the same time seeing that Lenin was transported safely through Germany in a sealed railway car into Russia, where Lenin and Trotsky Bolsheviks would oust Kerensky. In 1916, Lenin had proclaimed: "The aim of socialism is not only to abolish the present division of mankind into small states and all-national isolation, not only to bring the nations closer to each other, but also to merge them."

The key figure of Colonel House, whose father was a confidential agent in the U.S. for London banking interests (perhaps the Rothschilds), had close contacts with J. P. Morgan and Kuhn, Loeb & Co. Jacob Schiff from Frankfurt, Germany, was head of Kuhn, Loeb in the U.S. The Schiff family had ties with the Rothschilds for over a century, and Jacob Schiff heavily financed Woodrow Wilson's 1912 presidential campaign. In January 1916, Schiff paid Trotsky's way to the U.S., and on page two of the March 24, 1917, *New York Times,* a telegram of his was printed in which he described the successful Russian Revolution as "what we had hoped and striven for these long years." And the *New York Journal-American* (February 3, 1949) stated: "Today it is estimated even by Jacob's grandson, John Schiff, a prominent member of New York Society, that the old man sank about $20,000,000 for the final triumph of Bolshevism in Russia. Other New York banking firms also contributed."

After the Bolshevik triumph, Colonel House on November 28, 1917, cabled President Wilson from Paris that "there have been cabled over and published here statements made by American papers to the effect that Russia should be treated as an enemy. It is exceedingly important that such criticisms should be suppressed."

Regarding this, Skull & Bones member Charles Seymour (editor of *The Intimate Papers of Colonel House,* 1928) wrote that House was able "to prevent the formulation of a policy, demanded by certain groups among the French and British, of assisting the anti-Bolshevik factions in Russia; a policy, he believed, which would merely unite war-weary Russia behind the faction that offered peace."

Colonel House was a founding member of the CFR, as was Jacob Schiff's son, Mortimer, along with Jacob Schiff's partner, Paul Warburg (a CFR director from its founding, in 1921, until 1932). Warburg was a German banker, associated with the Rothschilds, who migrated to the U.S. in 1902 and soon became a partner in Kuhn, Loeb. He was also the architect of the Federal Reserve, which according to its supporter, Col. Elisha Ely Garrison (Skull & Bones member) in *Roosevelt, Wilson and the Federal Reserve Law* (1931), performed all the functions of a central bank, but was misnamed to mislead the public.

In the late 1800s, Garrison developed the concept of a "Federal Reserve," and in 1912 showed William Jennings Bryan how advocacy of a central bank could be sneaked into the Democratic Party platform upon which Woodrow Wilson would willingly run. Garrison would later say in his 1931 book that "with the help of Mr. Wu's mysterious letter I was to use those [Chinese bloc of] votes to swing a national election for President of the United States." The year before this book, an article appeared in the *New York Times* (June 1930) quoting Rep. Louis McFadden (chairman of the House Committee on Banking and Currency) as saying:

> The Federal Reserve Bank of New York is eager to enter into close relationship with the Bank for International Settlements. . . . The conclusion is impossible to escape that the State and Treasury Departments are willing to pool the banking system of Europe and America, setting up a world financial power independent of and above the Government of the United States. . . . The United States under present conditions will be transformed from the most active of manufacturing nations into a consuming and importing nation with a balance of trade against it.

Rep. McFadden was quoted in the *New York Times Magazine* (November 21, 1971) as further stating that the Federal Reserve Act set up "a world banking system . . . a super-state controlled by international bankers and international industrialists acting together to enslave the world for their own pleasure." In Congress on June 10, 1932, McFadden stated that "immense sums belonging to our national-bank depositors have been given to Germany on no collateral security whatsoever. . . . Billions and billions of our money has been pumped into Germany by the Federal Reserve Board." Then, in Congress on June 15, 1933, he noted that

> from the date of Trotsky's return to Russia the course of Russian history has, indeed, been greatly affected by the operations of international bankers. . . . The Soviet Government has been given United States Treasury funds by the Federal Reserve Board and the Federal Reserve banks acting through the Chase Bank . . . and other banks in New York City. . . . Shortly after Trotsky's arrival in Russia he was informed that he had a credit in Sweden at the Swedish branch of the bank owned by Max Warburg of Hamburg. This credit helped to finance the seizure of the Russian revolution.

The next year in Congress, McFadden explained that the Great Depression beginning in 1929 "was not accidental. It was a carefully contrived occurrence. . . . The international bankers sought to bring about a condition of despair here so they might emerge as rulers of us all." There were at least two attempts (by gunfire) on McFadden's life and he later died shortly after attending a banquet, causing some to suspect poisoning.

J. P. Morgan and company had pushed for the establishment of the Bank for International Settlements under the Hague Agreement in 1930, and it was J. P. Morgan who asked Paul Warburg to draw up the plan for the Federal Reserve. Warburg's daughter, Felicia Schiff Warburg (great-granddaughter of Jacob Schiff), would marry Robert Sarnoff, who would succeed his father, David Sarnoff (CFR member), who would head RCA (with its subsidiary NBC) with financial backing from Kuhn, Loeb and other banking firms connected with the Rothschilds.

Another American friendly to the Bolsheviks was Raymond Robins, sent to St. Petersburg in Russia to head the American Red Cross Mission shortly after the Bolsheviks gained power. He became friends with Bruce Lockhart, sent by Lloyd

George and Lord Alfred Milner (who carried out Cecil Rhodes' plans) to establish "unofficial relations with the Bolsheviks" for Britain. In Lockhart's book, *British Agent* (1933), he says about Robins (a protegé of Col. Edward M. House, about whom President Wilson said "his thoughts and mine are one," and who wrote in 1912 *Philip Dru: Administrator* promoting "Socialism as dreamed of by Karl Marx"):

> Although a rich man himself, he was an anti-capitalist. . . . Hitherto, his two heroes had been [Teddy] Roosevelt and Cecil Rhodes. Now Lenin captured his imagination. . . . Robins was the only man whom Lenin was always willing to see and who ever succeeded in imposing his own personality on the unemotional Bolshevik leader. . . . I returned from our interview to our flat to find an urgent message from Robins requesting me to come to see him at once. . . . When I arrived, he had just finished telephoning Lenin. He had delivered his ultimatum [about Saalkind, assistant commissar for foreign affairs]. . . . Then the telephone rang and Robins picked up the receiver. Lenin had capitulated. Saalkind was dismissed from his post.

This shows the power the world planners had over Lenin and the Bolsheviks.

Relevant to Lenin and the Bolsheviks in the U.S., prior to socialist-communist Roger Baldwin helping found the American Civil Liberties Union (ACLU) in 1920, he wrote a letter August 1917 to Louis Lochner, head of the Bolshevik "People's Council of America," stating:

> Do steer away from making it look like a Socialist enterprise. Too many people have already gotten the idea that it is nine-tenths a Socialist movement. You can, of course, avoid this by bringing to the front people like Senator Works, Miss Addams, and others, who are known as substantial Democrats. . . . We also want to look like patriots in everything we do. We want to get a lot of good flags, talk a good deal about the Constitution and what our forefathers wanted to make of this country.

In November 1918, though, Baldwin's friends published his statement that "in our own country the Non-Partisan League, radical labor and the Socialist Party hold the germs of a new social order. Their protest is my protest."

In the future, CFR members Arthur Schlesinger, Jr., Elmo Roper, and J. Robert Oppenheimer would be ACLU National Committee members. And CFR member Norman Cousins would be an ACLU board member (and World Federalist Association president), who would later say: "World government is coming, in fact, it is inevitable. No arguments for or against it can change that fact." This is similar to what CFR member James Warburg (Paul Warburg's son) would tell a congressional subcommittee February 17, 1950, when he said that "we shall have world government, whether or not we like it. The question is only whether world government will be achieved by consent or by conquest."

Returning again to Frankfurter, he would also help found the ACLU, after he resumed his law professorship at Harvard University. He had developed a close relationship with Franklin Roosevelt, about whom Rexford Tugwell wrote: "He had a good Harvard education when Fabianism was developing, and he probably knew quite well the works of H. G. Wells and George Bernard Shaw [Fabian socialists]."

President Franklin Roosevelt appointed Frankfurter to the U.S. Supreme Court in 1939; and reminiscent of Benjamin Disraeli's statement in his own novel *Coningsby* (1844) that "the world is governed by very different personages from what is imagined by those who are not behind the scenes," Curtis Dall (member of the N.Y. Stock Exchange and husband of Anna Roosevelt) related in *F.D.R.: My Exploited Father-in-Law* (1967) that Frankfurter would be quoted as saying, "The real rulers in Washington are invisible, and exercise power from behind the scenes." (Interestingly, on page A6832 of the *Congressional Record,* September 22, 1950, Congressman Martin Dies quoted FDR as saying to him: "I do not believe in communism any more than you do but there is nothing wrong with the Communists in this country; several of the best friends I have got are Communists.")

Dall also explained that the October 1929 stock market crash

> was the calculated "shearing" of the public by the World-Money powers, triggered by the planned sudden shortage of the supply of call money in the New York money market.... For a long time I felt that FDR had developed many thoughts and ideas that were his own to benefit this country, the U.S.A. But he didn't. Most

of his thoughts, his political "ammunition," as it were, was carefully manufactured for him in advance by the CFR-One-World Money group.

Perhaps that's why on November 21, 1933, FDR had written to former President Woodrow Wilson's closest adviser, Col. Edward M. House: "The real truth of the matter is, as you and I know, that a financial element in the larger centers has owned government ever since the days of Andrew Jackson."

What Dall wrote was supported by the October 26, 1935, edition of the *National Message* (found at the New York Public Library), where one reads: "It was told to me by a heavyweight American financier before the crash came, that the crash was coming; that it would be permitted to run to the danger point; and that then, when the danger point was passed, it would be reversed by measures carefully prepared in advance to meet the situation."

What Dall wrote was also supported by the comments of money baron Bernard Baruch in *Baruch: The Public Years* (1960), when he wrote:

> Nothing did more to spur the boom in stocks than the decision made by the New York Federal Reserve Bank, in the spring of 1927, to cut the rediscount rate. Benjamin Strong, Governor of the bank, was chief advocate of this unwise measure, which was taken largely at the behest of Montagu Norman of the Bank of England. . . . At the time of the Bank's action I warned of its consequences. . . . I felt that sooner or later the market had to break.

What Dall wrote was further supported by noted Australian William C. Wentworth, who wrote a letter-to-the-editor of *The Australian,* February 7, 1989, revealing that

> In 1929 I was a member of the Oxford and Cambridge athletic team, visiting America. . . . In July, we boarded a smallish passenger vessel in New York. . . . A fellow passenger was Montagu Norman [head of the Bank of England], returning to London, after a secret visit to the U.S. Central Bank, travelling incognito. . . . He asked us not to blow his cover, because if the details of his movement were made public, it could have serious financial consequences. . . . He said, "In the next few months there is going to be a shake-out. But don't worry—it won't last for long."

A few months later on October 29, the stock market crash began.

In Arthur Schlesinger, Jr.'s *The Coming of the New Deal* (1958), he quotes Machiavelli at the front of the book saying, "There is nothing . . . more dangerous to handle, than to initiate a new order of things."

And at the end of the book, he quotes Fabian socialist H. G. Wells describing FDR as "the most effective transmitting instrument possible for the coming of the new world order. . . . He is continuously revolutionary in the new way without ever provoking a stark revolutionary crisis."

Elsewhere in the book, he states regarding Henry A. Wallace (FDR's vice president 1941–45):

> the occult fascinated him . . . had drawn him in the late twenties into the orbit of a White Russian mystic in the tradition of Blavatsky named Dr. Nicholas Roerich . . . billing himself [Roerich] as the exclusive representative of the White Brotherhood of the East. . . . Wallace probably found release [or refuge] in Roerich's theosophical potpourri. . . . On one occasion, Wallace even rashly wrote Roosevelt: "I feel for a short time yet, that we must deal with . . . the 'flameless ones' who with one last dying gasp will strive to re-animate their dying giant 'Capitalism.' Mr. President, you can be the 'flaming one.' . . ."

In *Changing Esoteric Values* by Foster Bailey, on page 58, Colonel House is referred to as a "disciple" and President Wilson is referred to as a "sixth ray disciple." Foster's wife, Alice Bailey (the leading occultist of the day), referred to FDR as "that great first ray disciple," in *The Externalisation of the Hierarchy,* in which she wrote of those who "will develop the new world religion . . . [and] the new civilisation. . . . They can, however, be delayed by the reactionary types of people, by the ultra-conservative and closed minds. . . . These must all be brought under the power of death."

By "death" she meant the "power to relinquish," which is interesting given that Skull & Bones members William Howard Taft and George H. W. Bush relinquished the presidency in the similar elections of 1912 and 1992. In the August 7, 1988, front page *Washington Post* article, **"Bush opened up to Secret Yale Society,"** by Bob Woodward and Council on Foreign Relations (CFR) member Walter Pincus, is written: *"Memento Mori*—Latin for 'Remember that you must die.' It is one of the phrases that is part of the lore in the 156–year–old Skull & Bones ritual.... Bush's oldest son, George W. Bush, also was in Bones, Class of 1968, as were about a half-dozen other Bush family members." (George W. Bush in November 1994 would be elected Governor of Texas; in November 2000 he would be elected president of the U.S., and re–elected in 2004)

The socialist Christopher Hitchens (friend of Bill Clinton at Oxford University) explained in *The Nation* (December 14, 1992):

> A Rhodesian formation imparts a definite sense of knowing what is best . . . for others. It has helped bestow a patina of refinement on the raw exercise of power, and has shaped the contours of the permanent party of government as it exists in law, lobbying, business, intelligence, diplomacy and the military.... In his [George W. Bush's] establishment heart, he must have realized that nothing is more calculated than a Rhodes background to assure a smooth and equable transition.

George H. W. Bush's father, Prescott Bush, also had been a member of Skull & Bones, as had three of his partners in Brown Brothers, Harriman & Co. private bankers. Prescott was a director of the Columbia Broadcasting System (CBS) and had arranged the credit to allow William Paley to buy the network outright. Paley began CBS in 1928 and hired Sigmund Freud's nephew, Edward Bernays, as his chief adviser. In the same year of 1928, Bernays authored *Propaganda,* in which he revealed that:

> Those who manipulate the organized habits and opinions of the masses constitute an invisible government which is the true ruling power of the country.... It remains a fact that in almost every act of our daily lives, whether in the sphere of politics or business, in our social conduct or our ethical thinking, we are dominated by the relatively small number of persons.... It is they who pull the wires which control the public mind, who harness old social forces and contrive new ways to bind and guide the world.... As civilization has become more complex, and as the need for invisible government has been increasingly demonstrated, the technical means have been invented and developed by which opinion may be regimented.

One way of "manipulating opinion" was through the press, especially via new magazines such as *Time*, begun in the early 1920s by Henry Luce and Brit Hadden, both of whom in 1920 had been members of Skull & Bones, characterized in Robert Herzstein's biography *Henry R. Luce* (1994) as "a secretive group of young men pledged to help each other throughout their lives."

Herzstein also wrote that after Luce's father had met John D. Rockefeller, Jr., "early on, young Harry [Henry Luce] learned that a powerful circle of contacts and friends could move the world."

Ultimately, the "manipulation" would take the form of a dialectical process toward a world of synthesis. The thesis of western capitalism and the antithesis of eastern communism would synthesize into world socialism, as John Dewey (father of "Progressive Education") in *Individualism, Old and New* (1929) said:

> We are in for some kind of socialism, call it by whatever name we please, and no matter what it will be called when it is realized. . . . There is still enough vitality in the older individualism to offer a very serious handicap to any party or program which calls itself by the name Socialism. But in the long run, the realities of the situation will exercise control over the connotations which, for historical reasons, cling to a word. . . . The older individualism is still sufficiently ingrained to obtain allegiance in confused sentiment and in vocal utterance. It persists to such an extent that we can maintain the illusion that it regulates our political thought and behavior. In actuality, appeal to it serves to perpetuate the current disorganization in which financial and industrial power, corporately organized, can deflect economic consequences away from the advantage of the many to serve the privilege of the few. . . . The [political] parties have been eager accomplices in maintaining the confusion and unreality. . . . It testifies to the import of the crowd psychology of suggestion and credulity in American life. Christian Science rules American thought in business affairs; if we can be led to think that certain things do not exist [e.g., conspiracies] they perforce have not happened. . . . The problem of social [public] control of industry and the use of governmental agencies for constructive social ends will become the avowed center of political struggle. . . . No phase of our culture would remain unaffected. . . .

(See quotes from 1928 Dewey article on pages 115–116 of my book here.)

In *Democracy and Education* (1916), Dewey had earlier written that independent individualists have a "form of insanity." Then in 1932, Dewey was made honorary president of the National Education Association (NEA). And in that same year, the NEA's Department of Superintendence published its *Tenth Yearbook* entitled "Character Education," in which one could read that

> the objective of character education is to teach the child that he will do the best possible thing in each situation, old and new.... Relativity must replace absolutism in the realm of morals.... Loyalty to the family must be merged into loyalty to the community, loyalty to the community into loyalty to the nation, and loyalty to the nation into loyalty to mankind. The citizen of the future must be a citizen of the world.

Fabian socialist H. G. Wells explained the movement toward socialism further in *Experiment in Autobiography* (1934), when he commented: "The organization of this that I call the Open Conspiracy, the evocation of a greater sounder fellow to the Communist essay, an adequately implemented Liberal Socialism, which will ultimately supply teaching, coercive and directive public services to the whole world, is the immediate task."

He went on to say that when the planned world-state would finally be precipitated, "Its coming is likely to happen very quickly.... Sometimes I feel that generations of propaganda and education may have to precede it.... Plans for political synthesis seem to grow bolder and more extensive."

FDR wrote a letter February 13, 1935, to Wells concerning this book, saying:

> How do you manage to retain such extraordinarily clear judgements?... I believe our [FDR's administration] biggest success is making people think during these past two years. They may not think straight but they are thinking in the right direction—and your direction and mine are not so far apart; at least we both seek peaceable conveyances in our travels.

Two weeks later, Wells replied on February 27 that he would like to talk with FDR in

<u>COPY</u>

April 14th, 1934

Dear Mr President,

      You wrote me a very pleasant note some months ago.
These indiscretions carry their penalties.
I am profoundly interested in the world situation
and I want very much to have half an hour's conversation
with you. I am coming to America early in May on
the chance of being able to have that brief talk.
If I could talk to you <u>and to Mrs Roosevelt</u> all
sorts of things that are vague in my mind will
become definite. I am more and more persuaded
that you are in a key position in the world's affairs
and extraordinarily right-minded and right-spirited.
I have no intention of writing about any conversation
we may have, but I shall probably be writing articles
and talking on the air later, and I want to feel
that I'm as close to the personal reality of the
situation as I can.

      I shall probably come by the <u>Washington</u>, leaving
here on April 26th, and I do not intend to stay in
America for more than ten or twelve days. I've
talked to Roosevelt I, Harding and Hoover at
Washington and I shall be extremely grateful if you
can give me an appointment.

      Very sincerely Yours

      (SIGNED) H.G. Wells

I shall be on the <u>Washington</u> after April 26th and also
any letters to me at the Chase National Bank,
Park Avenue, New York will reach me.

THE WHITE HOUSE
WASHINGTON

February 13, 1935.

Personal

My dear Mr. Wells:-

  Your experiment in autobiography
was for me an experiment in staying awake instead
of putting the light out. How do you manage to
retain such vivid pictures of events and such
extraordinarily clear impressions and judgments?

  I do hope you will come over
again this year. We are still moving forward,
not only as a Government but very distinctly as
a people. I believe our biggest success is
making people think during these past two years.
They may not think straight but they are thinking in the right direction -- and your direction
and mine are not so far apart; at least we both
seek peaceable conveyances in our travels.

  With my sincere regards,

    Faithfully yours,

     Franklin D Roosevelt

H. G. Wells, Esq.,
47 Chilten Court,
London, N.W.,
England.

THE WHITE HOUSE
WASHINGTON

November 9, 1939

My dear Mr. Wells:

Thank you for sending me your proposed
"Declaration of the Rights of Man", which I have
read with great interest. It embodies many of
the fundamental rights of the individual expressed
in a form which cannot fail to meet with sym—
pathetic consideration among the democratic people
of the world.

Very sincerely yours,

Franklin D. Roosevelt

H. G. Wells, Esq.,
13, Hanover Terrace,
Regent's Park, N.W. 1,
London, England.

the U.S. in early March, and he gave as his address "c/o Chase National Bank, N.Y.C." (controlled by John D. Rockefeller). FDR had written Wells earlier on December 4, 1933, saying "I have read, with pleasure and profit, almost everything that you have written. . . . You are doing much to educate people everywhere, and for that I am grateful." And FDR would write Wells on November 9, 1939, thanking him for his proposed "Declaration of the Rights of Man," saying "It embodies many of the fundamental rights of the individual expressed in a form which cannot fail to meet with sympathetic consideration among the democratic people of the world."

In 1936, former Democratic presidential candidate Alfred E. Smith delivered a speech in Washington, D.C., titled "Betrayal of the Democratic Party." In 1932, Smith had supported FDR, but in this speech of January 25, 1936, he stated:

> Just get the platform of the Democratic Party, and get the platform of the Social-
> ist Party, and lay them down on your dining room table, side by side, and get a
> heavy lead pencil and scratch out the word "Democrat," and scratch out the word
> "Socialist," and let the two platforms lay there. Then study the record of the present
> Administration up to date. After you have done that, make your mind up to pick
> up the platform that more nearly squares with the record, and you will put your
> hand on the Socialist platform.

At the end of this same year, on November 20, 1936, H. G. Wells delivered an address titled "World Encyclopaedia" to the Royal Institution of Great Britain (see Wells' *World Brain,* 1938) in which he suggested "a new social organ[ization], a new institution" called "World Encyclopaedia" which

> would play the role of an undogmatic Bible to a world culture. . . . It would hold
> the world together mentally. . . . Ultimately, if our dream is realized, it must exert
> a very great influence upon everyone who controls administrations, makes wars,
> directs mass behavior, feeds, moves, starves and kills populations. . . . You see how
> such an Encyclopaedic organization could spread like a nervous network, a system
> of mental control about the globe.

Wells had described his "Open Conspiracy" (the inspiration for Marilyn Ferguson's 1980 *The Aquarian Conspiracy,* perhaps influenced by Willis Harman's May 1974

Stanford Research Institute study, *Changing Images*) in *Anticipations of the Reaction of Mechanical and Scientific Progress on Human Life and Thought* (1901) as the "New Republic" (new world order) which "will appear first as a conscious organization of intelligent and quite possibly in some cases wealthy men, as a movement having distinct social and political aims, confessedly ignoring most of the existing apparatus of political control, or using it only as an incidental implement in the attainment of these aims." Three years after *World Brain* was published, Wells wrote a letter to Winston Churchill (they both belonged to the same dining club), who replied to Wells on October 15, 1941: "Many thanks for your letter.... It is quite impossible for me to discuss these matters outside the secret circle" (the letter from Churchill is in the Rare Book Room of the University of Illinois Library at Urbana-Champaign).

The Fabian socialists had founded the London School of Economics in 1895 to train socialists for the government bureaucracy (and elsewhere) gradually to put into place their plan to "manage" society via rules and regulations. It was described as a slowly executed "plot" by Fabian socialist H. G. Wells in *New Worlds for Old* (1908). In Fabian Beatrice Webb's autobiography, *Our Partnership* (1948), she indicated that she and her husband received help from the Rothschilds to finance the London School of Economics. Then in 1920, Sir Ernest Cassel, associated with Kuhn, Loeb, donated £472,000 to the school when it was in serious financial trouble. And Prof. J. H. Morgan in *The Quarterly Review* (January 1929) wrote: "When I once asked Lord Haldane why he persuaded his friend, Sir Ernest Cassel, to settle by his will large sums on ... the London School of Economics, he replied, 'Our object is to make this institution a place to raise and train the bureaucracy of the future Socialist State.'"

The Fabians' plan extended to the U.S. and was described in Rose Martin's *Fabian Freeway* (1968) as follows:

> From 1931, Harold Ickes belonged to an elite corps calling itself the Government [later, National] Planning Association, which drafted the tentative blueprint for the New Deal in consultation with the Fabian-sponsored group in London known as PEP (Political and Economic Planning). ... On May 3, 1934, Congressman Louis McFadden [in the *Congressional Record,* pp. 8042–43] quoted Israel Moses Sieff as stating: "Let us go slowly for a while, until we can see how our plan works

out in America." Sieff belonged to the British organization PEP, and the plan to which he referred was the New Deal. . . . A PEP document issued in 1931, under the title *Freedom and Planning,* had recommended setting up National Councils in Agriculture, Transport and Coal Mining—resembling the industry-wide councils afterward set up in the U.S. under the National Recovery Act [of the New Deal]. The manufacturer was to be regulated through national planning. Waste in distribution was to be eliminated through a system of department and grocery store chains. The individual farmer would be told just what and how much he could plant. Large tracts of land were to be acquired by the Government. . . . A lineal descendant of both PEP and the National Planning Association is the Committee for Economic Development (CED) founded in 1941.

In the 1990s, CED will be composed of some 250 business leaders and educators, almost 100 of whom are CFR members. Its purpose is to propose policies, and one of its latest statements (1991) will be titled *The Unfinished Agenda: A New Vision for Child Development and Education.* Interesting also will be the fact that of 22 members of the board of directors of the New American Schools Development Corporation, five will be with the CED and seven with the CFR. Also a descendant of PEP would be PPBS (Planning-Programming-Budgeting System) instituted in the 1960s in the U.S. by Charles Hitch, assistant secretary of defense and comptroller during the presidency of Lyndon Johnson. Hitch had been a Rhodes Scholar in England in 1932–33 when PEP was being instituted.

In 1932, William Z. Foster (head of the Communist Party in America) wrote *Toward Soviet America* indicating the American Soviet government would have a "National Department of Education and its state and local branches. . . . Students would be taught on the basis of Marxian dialectical materialism, internationalism and the general ethics of the new socialist society."

About this same time, John Dewey's disciple, George Counts, wrote that "competition [must be replaced] by cooperation, trust in Providence by careful planning, and private capitalism by some form of socialized economy."

Similarly, the first *Humanist Manifesto* (1933, co-authored by John Dewey) called for "a socialized and cooperative economic order." One of the signers of the first *Humanist Manifesto* was C. F. Potter, who in 1930 wrote *Humanism: A New*

NATIONAL PLANNING BOARD

FEDERAL EMERGENCY ADMINISTRATION
OF PUBLIC WORKS
HAROLD L. ICKES, Administrator

FINAL REPORT—1933–34

MEMBERS OF THE BOARD
FREDERIC A. DELANO, Chairman
CHARLES E. MERRIAM   WESLEY C. MITCHELL

UNITED STATES GOVERNMENT PRINTING OFFICE   WASHINGTON : 1934

Religion, in which he said, "Education is thus a most powerful ally of humanism. What can the theistic Sunday schools, meeting for an hour once a week, and teaching only a fraction of the children, do to stem the tide of a five-day program of humanistic teaching?"

In 1934, the year after the first *Humanist Manifesto* was published, Willard Givens (who would become executive secretary of the National Education Association in 1935) wrote that a dying *laissez-faire* must be completely destroyed and all of us, including the "owners," must be subjected to a large degree of social control. . . . An equitable distribution of income will be sought. . . . And the major function of the school is social orientation of the individual. It must seek to give him understanding of the transition to a new social order.

Givens held his NEA position for seventeen years and then took over the education program of the Supreme Council 33rd degree of the Scottish Rite Freemasons. Also pertaining to Freemasonry, psychiatrist Dr. Robert Felix joined the Federal Public Health Service in 1933, helped develop the Mental Health Act of 1946, and from 1975 to 1985 was research director of the Freemasons' Scottish Rite Psychophrenic Research Program. Relatedly, the year after the Mental Health Act of 1946, the Delaware State Society for Mental Hygiene (with acknowledgements to the Supreme Council, Scottish Rite Masons, Northern Jurisdiction) published in 1947 (the same year the Tavistock Institute of Human Relations in London and the Research Center for Group Dynamics in the U.S. began publishing the journal *Human Relations*) the book, *Human Relations in the Classroom, Course I,* in the preface of which one finds that "in 1932, the president of the Carnegie Foundation for the Advancement of Teaching said to Dr. C. M. Hincks, distinguished psychiatrist, 'You, in the mental hygiene field are making little real progress with educators.'"

Also relevant to Carnegie at this time, the Carnegie Corporation gave $340,000 toward the work of the Commission on Social Studies of the American Historical Association. In 1934, the Commission published its "Conclusions and Recommendations" in the form of a report which philosopher of British socialism Harold Laski would later characterize as follows: "At bottom, and stripped of its carefully neutral phrases, the report is an educational program for a socialist America" (see *The New Republic,* July 29, 1936).

George Counts was research director for the Commission, and in its "Conclusions and Recommendations" was written: "American civilization, in common with Western Civilization, is passing through one of the great critical stages of history, is modifying its traditional faith in economic individualism, and is embarking upon vast experiments in social planning and control which call for large-scale co-operation on the part of the people."

Not only would this economic and political planning be synthesized, but John Dewey in *Common Faith* (1934) also proposed a syncretization or synthesis of the world's faiths or religions. A decade later in *Discipleship in the New Age* (1944), occultist Alice Bailey would characterize "the new world religion" as a "synthesis" by "illuminators of group thought." And to show how religion, politics, and economics were all included, *Time* (March 16, 1942) reported that John Foster Dulles was chairman of a Federal Council of Churches meeting in early March 1942 that recommended limitations on national sovereignty, a world government, international control of armies, a universal system of money, and elimination of tariffs and quota restrictions on trade. They referred to "a new order of economic life" and that "every individual [has an] obligation to work in some socially necessary service."

World Council of Churches co-secretary William Paton said, "Collectivism is coming, whether we like it or not."

According to the *New York Times* (October 29, 1939), Dulles (a CFR founder) had already delivered a speech (October 28) to the YMCA in which he stated:

> Some dilution or leveling off of the sovereignty system . . . must take place to the immediate disadvantage of those nations which now possess the preponderance of power. . . . the establishment of a common money might be vested in a body created by and responsible to the principal of trading and investing peoples. This would deprive our government of exclusive control over a national money. . . .

Dulles would represent the World Council of Churches at the U.N. Festival of All Faiths in San Francisco on June 19, 1955. He was secretary of state, and his brother Allen Dulles was head of the CIA, and both were members of World Brotherhood as well as the Council on Foreign Relations. This was the same year (1955) that Erich Fromm's *The Sane Society* was published, in which he predicted that

> the theistic concepts are bound to disappear in the future development of humanity. . . . A new religion will develop . . . the most important feature of such a religion would be its universalistic character . . . it would embrace the humanistic teachings common to all great religions of the East and of the West. . . . The same suggestion for a new humanistic religion has been made by Julian Huxley in "Evolutionary Humanism," *The Humanist,* Vol. XII, 5, 1952, p. 201 ff.

Because of the sectarian nature of most religions, however, a synthesis would not occur easily, and therefore a surrogate "religion" would provide an intermediate stage on the way to a "common faith." Abraham Maslow called his Third Force Humanistic Psychology "the new 'religion' surrogate . . . [and] the equivalent of a 'religious' seminary to train 'ministers.'" Everything would be sacralized based upon what he called Eupsychian principles leading to self-actualization (and finding "the divine" within oneself). He said these could be used to "manage" countries, or corporations, or churches, and in his April 17, 1962, entry in *The Journals of A. H. Maslow,* he records: "Very 'successful' lecture last night before hundreds of Catholics. They shouldn't applaud me—they should attack. If they were fully aware of what I was doing, they would."

One Catholic, Avery Dulles (John Foster Dulles' son), was a Jesuit priest on the board of directors of Georgetown University (1966–1968) during Bill Clinton's last years there before Clinton became a Rhodes Scholar at Oxford University.

Maslow's journal entry above was at the same time Arthur Schlesinger, Jr. was a special assistant to President John F. Kennedy. Schlesinger had written in the May–June 1947 *Partisan Review* that "there seems no inherent obstacle to the gradual advance of socialism in the United States through a series of New Deals. . . The transition must be piecemeal; it must be parliamentary."

For the "gradual advance" toward world socialism to occur, though, a major new educational program would be necessary. The *Syracuse (N.Y.) Post-Standard* (February 16, 1947) had reported University of Chicago instructor Milton Mayer as saying, "We must haul down the American flag, and if I wanted to be vulgar and shocking, I would go even farther and say, haul it down, stamp on it and spit on it." Separately and later that same year, in December 1947, *A Report of the President's (Truman) Commission on Higher Education* was released, stating:

> There is urgent need for a program of education for world citizenship that can be made a part of every person's general education. . . . It will take social science and social engineering to solve the problems of human relations. . . . The competitive principle must give place to the principle of cooperation. . . . East and West are coming together in one world order. We could not stem this development if we wanted to.

Of course, this was acceptable to President Harry S. Truman who had already agreed on April 6, 1946, that a new course should be instituted in the high school curriculum to prepare youth for world citizenship (almost fifty years later, *United Nations fiftieth anniversary,* Summer 1995, Issue 6, promoted a "Passport to the Future" to "sign on millions of young persons as 'global citizens'"). Before that, he had said on June 28, 1945: "We are going to have to ratify this [U.N.] Constitution of San Francisco. . . . It will be just as easy for nations to get along in a republic of the world as it is for us to get along in the republic of the United States." On the same day, regarding the Charter of the World Court signed also at San Francisco, Truman said if two American states have a quarrel, "they bring suit in the Supreme Court and abide by its decision. There isn't a reason in the world why we can't do that internationally." And addressing the U.N. General Assembly (October 24, 1950), Truman proclaimed: "The United Nations represents the idea of a universal morality, superior to the interests of individual nations. . . . The men who laid down their lives for the United Nations in Korea. . . . They died in order that the United Nations might live."

A possible example of "social science and social engineering solving the problems of human relations" was found in Fabian socialist Bertrand Russell's *The Impact of Science on Society* (1953), where he stated that

> I think the subject which will be of most importance politically is mass psychology. . . . Various results will soon be arrived at: that the influence of home is obstructive . . . that verses set to music and repeatedly intoned are very effective [rock and roll music would come to be known for its "repeatedly intoned" verses and music]. . . . It may be hoped that in time anybody will be able to persuade anybody of anything if he can reach the patient young and is provided by the State with money and equipment. . . . Although this science will be diligently studied, it will be rigidly confined to the governing class. The populace will not be allowed to know how its convictions were generated. When the technique has been perfected, every government that has been in charge of education for a generation will be able to control its subjects securely without the need of armies or policemen. . . . A good society by which I believe that democratic socialism should be guided. . . . Competition will be effectively regulated by law, and mitigated by

government controls [e.g., NAFTA, GATT and the World Trade Organization]. ... Educational propaganda, with government help, could achieve this result in a generation. There are, however, two powerful forces opposed to such a policy: one is religion; the other is nationalism.... Population can be kept from increasing.... Perhaps bacteriological war may prove effective. If a Black Death could be spread throughout the world once in every generation survivors could procreate freely without making the world too full [heavily populated India had an outbreak of the plague in 1994]. ... A scientific world society cannot be stable unless there is a world government.... This authority should deal out the world's food to the various nations in proportion to their population at the time of the establishment of the authority. If any nation subsequently increased its population, it should not on that account receive any more food.

(Russell had written a letter to H. G. Wells on September 12, 1933, describing Russell's Beacon Hill School, and saying "the social synthesis is the important thing, and this is what our children are grappling with. We *are* the new planned society in miniature.")

In *War or Peace* (1950), John Foster Dulles declared: "I have never seen any proposal made for collective security with 'teeth' in it, or for 'world government' or for 'world federation,' which could not be carried out either by the United Nations or under the United Nations Charter."

And in an April 11, 1952, speech to the American Bar Association, Dulles proclaimed:

Treaties make international law and they also make domestic law. Under our Constitution, treaties become the supreme law of the land. They are, indeed, more supreme than ordinary laws for congressional laws are invalid if they do not conform to the Constitution, whereas treaty law can override the Constitution. Treaties, for example, can take powers away from the Congress and give them to the President; they can take powers from the States and give them to the Federal Government or to some international body, and they can cut across the rights given the people by their constitutional Bill of Rights.

As an example of how the Hegelian dialectic worked in synthesizing western capitalism and eastern communism into a world socialism, in 1953 a congressional research director, Norman Dodd, was told by Ford Foundation president H. Rowan Gaither that the foundation's personnel was continuing to operate "under directives from the White House to so alter life in America as to make possible a comfortable merger with the Soviet Union."

Gaither said this was a continuation of an attitude held by certain American government officials during the Second World War. And one example of the "comfortable" relationship that existed between these officials and the Soviets was given by FDR's assistant Harry Hopkins (in charge of Lend-Lease) in a June 1944 speech where he said: "The American people are bound to the people of the Soviet Union in the great alliance of the United Nations. We are determined that nothing shall stop us from sharing with you all that we have. . . ."

And he literally meant "all," because Major George Racey Jordan (a key figure in the Lend-Lease program) wrote in *From Major Jordan's Diaries* (1952) that Hopkins had approved sending the Soviets uranium and other critical material in the development of atomic weapons even before the U.S. had an atomic bomb completed! Relevant to this is the fact that on the first two pages of Brian Crozier's *Free Agent* (1993), he says that Harry Hopkins (personal adviser to FDR) was a fully paid Soviet agent recruited into the Soviet's NKVD for the purpose of convincing FDR that the Soviets had no aims to take Eastern Europe. Therefore, FDR did *not* support Churchill's plan for Allied Forces to move through Italy early into Eastern Europe before the Soviets could get there.

H. G. Wells had written in *The Shape of Things to Come* (1933) that the plan for a new world order would succeed on its third attempt (coming out of something that would occur in Basra, Iraq) around 1980, and that at that time, "Russia is ready to assimilate. Is eager to assimilate."

In *The New World Order* (1939), Wells proposed a "collectivist one-world state" comprised of "socialist democracies," and stated: "It is the system of nationalist individualism that has to go. . . . We are living in the end of the sovereign states. . . . In the great struggle to evoke a Westernized World Socialism, contemporary governments may vanish. . . . Countless people . . . will hate the new world order . . . and will die protesting against it."

At about the time Wells' prediction was supposed to come to fruition, Soviet leader Mikhail Gorbachev would write *Perestroika* (1987) revealing that "the essence of *perestroika* lies in the fact that *it unites socialism with democracy* and revives the Leninist concept of socialist construction both in theory and in practice. . . . We want more socialism."

In addressing the U.N. on December 7 of the next year, he called for "a new world order." And according to the *New York Times* (August 23, 1991), Gorbachev said upon returning to Moscow following the failed coup attempt: "I am convinced that socialism is correct. I'm an adherent of socialism."

According to the March 1995 *McAlvany Intelligence Advisor,* Vladimir Zhiri-novsky on November 9, 1994, at a press conference at the U.N. said, "There has long been a hidden agenda to merge America and Russia under the New World Order."

Members of Congress concerned about the increasing promotion of world citizenship and world government held Senate hearings on June 17, 1952, during which Major General Sumter Lowry (retired) testified that Department of State Publication number 4289 ("The United Nations and You") "makes the flat statement that our survival as men and women is dependent on the United Nations, which statement is not proper or true. . . . Small groups which take the lead from the State Department . . . are largely responsible for teaching the idea of world citizenship and the world socialistic state (government) in the schools." He then quoted prominent Florida banker George Lewis II as stating (*Tampa Tribune,* May 15, 1952) that world fellowship "will be promoted by world citizenship and protected by world federal government when we get it," and a *Clearwater Sun* editorial proclaiming "the day of nationalism is as extinct as the roc and the dodo bird," and Milton Eisenhower (former chairman of the United States Commission for UNESCO) stating, "It is in this light that we should view our latest attempt to create a true world government" (Department of State publication "UNESCO Leaders Speak"). Major General Lowry closed by asserting, "The State Department is the fountainhead of a movement to sell world government and world citizenship to our people." Congress voted on July 10, 1952, for Public Law 495, section 112 of which read: "None of the funds appropriated in this title ('Department of State Appropriation Act, 1953') shall be used for the promotion, direct or indirect, of the principles or doctrine of one world government or one world citizenship."

Despite the fact that on June 19, 1955, on "Meet the Press," U.S. Ambassador to the U.N. Henry Cabot Lodge, Jr., said he thought 11 percent of the rank-and-file Democrats and Republicans "want world government," the language adopted by Congress on July 10, 1952, appeared decade after decade until the Department of State Appropriation Act of 1987 when it was deleted. Then, it would be time for the development of the new world order to move into high gear.

Early the next year, February 1–5, 1988, the Soviet-American Citizens' Summit was held in this country. It was primarily the work of two women, New Age networker Barbara Marx Hubbard and Rama Vernon, the latter of whom said the idea for the summit came out of a meeting in Moscow of the Soviet Peace Committee in August 1986. According to a 1985 State Department report on Soviet "Active Measures," the SPC is linked to the Soviet Central Committee's International Department, which was created by Stalin to carry out subversion within other countries. Vernon went on to say regarding the summit that Anselm Rothschild (of the Rothschild banking family) "organized the program."

George H. W. Bush would run for the presidency of the United States in 1988, and on February 10, the *Washington Post* quoted David Rockefeller as remarking that "he's [Bush] one of us ['the Establishment']. . . . If he were president, he would be in a better position than anyone else to pull together the people in the country who believe that we are in fact living in one world and have to act that way."

In his acceptance speech at the Republican National Convention, George H. W. Bush spoke of "points of light" and of making the U.S. "a kinder and gentler nation." This was reminiscent of Freemasons like George Washington and Alexander Hamilton who spoke to each other using the term "points of light." And it was reminiscent of Masonic author Joseph Fort Newton, who wrote that "Freemasonry's simplicity, its dignity, and its spirituality sustain me . . . to make a gentler, kinder and wiser world in which to live."

The nineteenth century revolutionary Giuseppe Mazzini had been referred to at that time as an "established point of light when rays traversed the world." And in the early twentieth century, the occultist Alice Bailey wrote about "points of light" and a "new world order." Hindus refer to chakras "from the root center to the lotus of a thousand petals at the top of the head." And the theosophists (neo-Hindus) refer to the chakras as "points of light," which at the top of the head would be "a thousand points of light." President Bush's speech mentioning "a thousand points of light" and a "new world order" was written in the middle of the summer in 1988, but many months before, Linda Sexton's somewhat esoteric novel *Points of Light* was published by Little, Brown and Company, and was reviewed in the *New York Times* Book Review section (page 7) on January 24, 1988. At the front of the book, Sexton referred to Vincent van Gogh's quote referring to "points of light." And in W. H. Auden's "September 1, 1939," one reads: "Ironic points of light flash out wherever the Just exchange their messages: may I, composed like them of Eros and of dust beleaguered by the same negation and despair show an affirming flame."

Coincidently, Karl Marx's Communist League sprang from an organization called the League of the Just.

Regarding "the Establishment" of which George H. W. Bush and George W. Bush are members, a book was written about some of its leaders and was titled *The Wise Men* (1986). It was co-authored by Rhodes Scholar, CFR member, and a *Time* editor, Walter Isaacson, who described how six leaders "shaped a new world order," were internationalists, and had a "common outlook." One of them, Chip Bohlen, was quoted as saying about socialism, "maybe that is the road we ought to go down."

In the book, one also reads that Arthur Schlesinger, Jr. in 1965 wrote: "The New York financial and legal community was the heart of the American establishment . . . its front organizations, the Rockefeller, Ford and Carnegie foundations and the Council on Foreign Relations."

Remember that supposedly conservative President Richard Nixon (CFR member) shocked television newscaster Howard K. Smith in a January 6, 1971, interview when Nixon revealed that he was "now a Keynesian in economics" (John Maynard Keynes was a Fabian socialist).

The globalists in the "financial community" had already had a boost when President Ronald Reagan at the Economic Summit in Williamsburg, Virginia, pronounced in 1983 that "national economies need monetary coordination mechanisms, and that is why an integrated world economy needs a common monetary standard. . . . But, no national currency will do—only a world currency will work."

However, for a world socialist government to be established, the U.N. would have to be strengthened. Former British prime minister Margaret Thatcher in an address (December 12, 1997) before the Heritage Foundation's "Leadership for America" gala in Washington, DC, remarked:

> Today's international policy makers have succumbed to a liberal contagion whose most alarming symptom is to view any new and artificial structure as preferable to a traditional and tested one.... Their short-term goal is to subordinate American and other national sovereignties to multilateral authorities; their long-term goal, one suspects, is to establish the U.N. as a kind of embryo world government.

Pope Paul VI had already written *Populorum Progressio* (March 26, 1967) calling for "a new juridical order" and stating:

> As we told the United Nations General Assembly in New York: "Your vocation is to bring not just some peoples but all peoples together as brothers. . . . Who can fail to see the need and importance of thus gradually coming to the establishment of a world authority capable of taking effective action on the juridical and political planes?" . . . Delegates to international organizations, public officials, gentlemen of the press, teachers and educators—all of you must realize that you have your part to play in the construction of a new world order.

Then in 1990, Iraq's invasion of Kuwait offered the U.N. a good opportunity with George H. W. Bush and "the Establishment" to begin enforcement of the new world order. Curiously, the ruthless Saddam Hussein released a large number of American hostages (who, if he had placed them at key targets around Iraq, may have prevented the Allied attack against his country), freeing Bush to begin military action which would facilitate the beginning of the new world order. (On February 5, 1998, President Clinton would say: "Would the Iraqi people be better off if there were a change in Iraqi leadership? I certainly think they would be. But that is not what the U.N. has authorized us to do.")

But there was still a great need to establish a clear precedent for U.N. intervention in the internal affairs of a country in the form of nation-building. This was despite the fact that Article 2, Section 7 of the U.N. Charter states: "Nothing contained in the present Charter shall authorize the United Nations to intervene in matters which are essentially within the domestic jurisdiction of any state [nation]."

Somalia (1992–93) looked like the best prospect for U.N. nation-building, and on October 19, 1993, President Clinton said: "Right now we are engaging in a political process to see how we can resolve our mission in Somalia and to do all the things the United Nations ordered to do. . . ." However, the warlords in Somalia had other ideas, and the next best prospect was Haiti (1994). When President Clinton addressed the American public about the possibility of our leading a multinational force to invade Haiti, he stated that they would be carrying out "the will of the United Nations." For Clinton to order American troops to prepare to fight and die in Haiti was curious, given that in his letter about twenty-five years ago explaining his position on Vietnam, he indicated that no American should be asked to fight unless there was a direct and immediate threat to the national security of the U.S. itself.

President Clinton's reasons for proposing military action in Haiti were also curious. He said that we needed to remove the dictators there, restore democracy, and cited the closeness of Haiti to the mainland U.S. But why didn't liberals take the same position regarding Daniel Ortega in Nicaragua, instead of refusing even to help the Contras who weren't asking the U.S. to invade? Next, President Clinton pointed to all of the atrocities by the military dictators in Haiti. But that raises the questions of why he supported Most Favored Nation status for China after the atrocities by the dictators there! And why did the U.S. back the defrocked priest, Jean-Bertrand Aristide, given his support of brutal necklacing and his undemocratic actions concerning judges and the parliament in Haiti after his election? Clinton said it's because he got 70 percent of the vote of the Haitian people. Does that mean Clinton believes Richard Nixon should have stayed in power despite what he did because Nixon had received the overwhelming vote of the American people over George McGovern?

Of course, on September 18, a deal was made that avoided a military invasion of Haiti. American forces would be involved in a peacekeeping operation there, though, and therefore still be at risk. However, supposing that everything went smoothly, what actually happened and what was the message sent around the world? The message was that if military dictators removed a democratically elected government, looted and pillaged the country, raping the people, and shedding their blood everywhere, the worst thing that would happen to them would be that they'd be allowed to have a ton of money and be given amnesty for all of their atrocities. To world government advocates, though, this didn't matter because the U.N. was now running a country—a dream they had been looking for a long time, and which set an important precedent for future U.N. interventions in countries' internal affairs.

Intervention in American affairs could come in the form of developing standards for our military, as a recent document titled *Peace-Keeping Criminal Justice Standards for Military Police, U.S. Marine Corps* has inside the front cover a U.N. insignia and the title *United Nations Criminal Justice Standards for Peace-Keeping Police* with the statement that it was prepared by the Crime Prevention and Criminal Justice Branch of the U.N. Office at Vienna. In the 1970s, the U.S. Army contracted with humanist Sidney Simon for "an experimental program to change attitudes and behavior of 12,000 soldiers. . . ." And separately in March 1978, the U.S. Army developed a course entitled "Psychological Operations in Support of Special Forces Operations" (published by the Special Warfare Center at Fort Bragg, NC), lesson three of which describes how to change core attitudes, values, and behavior, and refers to humanist psychology father Abraham Maslow's hierarchical process.

On May 3, 1994, President Clinton signed Presidential Decision Directive 25, which has still only been released to top administration officials and a few members of Congress, and which strengthens the U.N. and describes how American soldiers will serve under foreign commanders. Could this all be relevant to the recent "Combat Arms Survey" created and conducted by Navy officer Lt. Commander Guy Cunningham asking three hundred Marines at the Twentynine Palms Marine Base in California as to their willingness to serve under U.N. command and fire on fellow Americans if they resist gun confiscations? And possibly relevant to this was a three-week exercise beginning April 22, 1994, and called Agile Provider 94, which was conducted in several southern U.S. states by soldiers from the U.S., France, the Netherlands, and Surinam, training in "forcible entry" among other things. (August 6–28, 1995, for the first time on U.S. soil, soldiers from the former Warsaw Pact held "peacekeeping exercises" with NATO soldiers.) More than "forcible entry," the *Chicago Sun-Times* (June 13–14, 1995) reported that helicopters from the U.S. Army Special Operations Command at Fort Bragg, NC, flew to two Chicago suburbs, in a multi-jurisdictional training exercise at low level at night, without forewarning the public. There was gunfire, and explosions, windows in homes rattled, and an abandoned seminary was hit to "give the pilots a chance to train in an urban environment," a Defense Department spokesman said.

Perhaps in "preventative peacekeeping" if American soldiers are unwilling to "forcibly enter" the homes of fellow Americans who are unwilling to have their guns confiscated, foreign troops on American soil would be willing. Would this be a possible concern if foreign troops were ever *permanently* stationed in the U.S.? Interesting in that regard may be the fact that on May 11, 1991, the *Dallas Morning News* (and other newspapers around the nation) reported that "German lawmakers and U.S. officials reacted favorably to the idea of a permanent German military presence" in the U.S. An organization in the U.S. called Jews for the Preservation of Firearms Ownership compiled a chart titled "Major 20th-Century Genocides: The Cost of 'Gun Control,'" showing that prior to committing genocide, Ottoman Turkey, the USSR, Nazi Germany, China, Uganda, and Cambodia all passed strong gun control laws. For example, just prior to Uganda's 1971–1979 genocide against Christians and political rivals, "The Firearms Act of 1970" was passed. Could something similar happen in America? Founding father George Mason warned: "To disarm the people is the best and most effectual way to enslave them." And patriot and scholar Noah Webster wrote, "Before a standing army can rule, the people must be disarmed as they are in almost every kingdom in Europe. The supreme power in America cannot enforce unjust laws by the sword because the whole body of the people are armed."

Or intervention in the U.S. could come also through UNICEF, which is now televising an ad here that ends with the words, "Every child is our child." Can't you just see a poster with a U.N.-blue-clothed, fierce-looking woman acting as the "global nanny" and pointing at the children of the world, saying like Uncle Sam that "Aunt Uni wants you!"

Or intervention could come through U.N. treaties such as the proposed Treaty on Global Warming. U.S. Senator Chuck Hagel, just back from the U.N. Global Warming Conference in Kyoto, Japan, appeared on CBS' "Face the Nation," December 14, 1997. On the program, Sen. Hagel, who chairs the Senate subcommittee monitoring global warming, said:

> The consequences of the actions that are taken, and if in fact we would move forward and ratify this treaty, are about our jobs, our economic future, our economic

growth, international competitiveness, national sovereignty. For example, for the first time in the history of America, we would be allowing a U.N. bureaucracy to come in and administer and enforce shutdowns of industries, business, farmers.

Or intervention could come through the United Nations Convention on the Rights of the Child. Early in 1993, Rhodes Scholars Bill Bradley (D-NJ) and Richard Lugar (R-IN), among others, introduced Senate Resolution 70, which stated:

> Whereas on November 20, 1989, the United States and other members of the United Nations unanimously endorsed the United Nations Convention on the Rights of the Child and urged national governments to ratify the Convention and make possible the application of the Convention as *international law;* Whereas the Convention, if implemented, will help establish *universal legal standards* for the care and protection of children against neglect, exploitation, and abuse; . . . the Convention remains a force for improving the lot of children, both *in the United States* and abroad . . . [emphasis added].

The specific provisions for children's "rights" contained within the Convention, and which would be applied to American children, are ominously destructive of parental authority. An example of this attitude expressed in plain language can be found in an April 12, 1982, Omaha, Nebraska, interview on Channel 6 when State Senator (later, Congressman) Peter Hoagland declared: "What we are most interested in, of course, are the children themselves. . . . We don't think that [the members of a religious flock] should be entitled to impose decisions or religious philosophies on their children, which could seriously undermine those children's ability to deal in this complicated world when they grow up."

The combination of promoting socialism along with world government as well as intervening in families on behalf of children is best demonstrated by Mortimer Adler, who has been a member of the World Federalists, a founder of the Aspen Institute for Humanistic Studies, and chairman of *Encyclopaedia Britannica.* In his *The Paideia Proposal* (1982), one reads that "the sooner a democratic society intervenes to remedy the cultural inequality of homes and environments, the sooner it will succeed in fulfilling the democratic mandate of equal educational opportunity for all."

Members of his Paideia Group included Carnegie Foundation president Ernest Boyer, who in January 1988 said that schools should no longer be seen as academic centers but should be turned into "social service centers," that school-based health clinics should be combined with day-care facilities, and that schools should assume the responsibility for feeding students all three meals a day since they would be in the school building from 7:00 a.m. to 6:30 p.m. And Coalition of Essential Schools head Ted Sizer (also a member of the Paideia Group) wrote in *Five Lectures . . . on Moral Education* (1970) that "Christian sermonizing denies individual autonomy, which . . . lies at the heart of a new morality . . . toward which we are to guide ourselves and other people. . . . Clearly, the strict adherence to a 'code' is out of date."

The National Paideia Center (an outgrowth of *The Paideia Proposal*) was founded in 1988 at UNC-Chapel Hill. And in *Haves Without Have-Nots* (1991), Adler advocated a socialist world government called the Union of Socialist Democratic Republics (USDR).

A brief history of the internationalizing of education has been provided in *The People vs. The Educational Confederacy* (1995) by O. Jerome Brown, Katherine Levans, and Chey Simonton, from whom most of the information in this paragraph comes. The International Bureau of Education (IBE) began (with a grant from the Rockefeller Foundation) in 1925 under a reorganization of the Rousseau Society of France. IBE and UNESCO held an "International Conference on Public Education" in 1949 at which Recommendation 28 undermined successful phonics methods by stating "the phonetic method . . . begins with separate elements (e.g., sounds, letters and symbols) of little significance to the child mind." In 1966, UNESCO officials endorsed the concept of lifelong education, after Paul Lengrand's paper "Introduction to Life-Long Education" was delivered to UNESCO in 1965. In 1971, UNESCO's Secretariat asked George Parkyn to "outline a possible model" for an education system based upon lifelong learning, and to develop "a means for bringing an existing national school system into line with lifelong learning." The result was Parkyn's *Towards a Conceptual Model of Life-long Education* (1971) indicating "radical changes in the entire social structure" would be needed for lifelong learning. For example, "infant health centers" would be needed. Parents and others would come to schools to "demonstrate skills." Students would participate in "community service," choose a vocational field and work part-time, and receive "certificates" of educational attainment. And a "national board of education" would draw up national policy. (Does this sound like what's been proposed for the U.S. today?) On July 7, 1975, UNESCO's director-general delivered an address, "UNESCO and the establishment of a new world order," calling for "the establishment of a new international economic, and even social and political, order" (*UNESCO Chronicle,* September 1975). In 1976, UNESCO published *Foundations of Lifelong Education,* which states that

> education should aim not so much at acquisition of knowledge... [today] there is less need to know the content of information.... [There should be a] transformation of life in its totality... [a] profound commitment to social tasks.... Achievements of socialist countries... have laid the foundation of a way of life which makes everyone understand its [sic] individual relevance ... [whereas capitalism] lays the foundations of rivalry and aggression and encourages exaggerated consumption, [making] man a slave of ambition and status symbols.... [Lifelong learning promotes] equality of end result, and not merely of opportunity... [and] fosters equality in terms of opinions, aspirations, motivations, and so on.... There is a dilemma—if lifelong education were to be based on the aim of increasing the yield of business enterprises and economic growth, it would merely serve to establish a totalitarian, one-dimensional society.

In 1980, UNESCO published *Educational Goals* as one book in the IBE's "Studies and Surveys in Comparative Education" series, and these goals would ultimately result in the goals adopted by the UNESCO-sponsored World Conference on Education for All (in 1990, about the same time and similar to the "National Educational Goals" developed in the U.S.).

Before children can be internationalized, however, they would have to be nationalized in socialism. That was projected in a widely used social service textbook written by Arthur Calhoun and titled *A Social History of the American Family* (vol. 3, 1919), in which he commented:

> The modern individual is a world citizen. . . . As familism weakens, society has to assume a larger parenthood. The school begins to assume responsibility for the functions thrust upon it. . . . The kindergarten grows downward toward the

cradle and there arises talk of neighborhood nurseries. . . . Social centers replace the old time home chimney. . . . The child passes more and more into the custody of community experts. . . . It seems clear that at least in its early stages, socialism will mean an increased amount of social control. . . . We may expect in the socialist commonwealth a system of public educational agencies that will begin with the nursery and follow the individual through life.

The objective would be to educate youth through social change to accept the autocratic state, and in 1968, Warren Bennis and Philip Slater wrote in *The Temporary Society:*

One cannot permit submission to parental authority if one wishes to bring about profound social change. . . . In order to effect rapid changes, any such centralized regime must mount a vigorous attack on the family lest the traditions of present generations be preserved. It is necessary, in other words, artificially to create an experiential chasm between parents and children to insulate the latter in order that they can more easily be indoctrinated with new ideas. The desire may be to cause an even more total submission to the state, but if one wishes to mold children in order to achieve some future goal, one must begin to view them as superior, inasmuch as they are closer to this future goal. One must also study their needs with care in order to achieve this difficult preparation for the future. One must teach them not to respect their tradition-bound elders, who are tied to the past and know only what is irrelevant.

The next year (1969), the Joint Commission on Mental Health of Children presented its report to Congress, stating:

As the home and church decline in influence . . . schools must begin to provide adequately for the emotional and moral development of children. . . . The school . . . must assume a direct responsibility for the attitudes and values of child development. The child advocate, psychologist, social technician, and medical technician should all reach aggressively into the community, send workers out to children's homes, recreational facilities, and schools. They should assume full responsibility for all education, including pre-primary education.

Radical feminists were only too willing to go along with this attitude, as two years later (1971), *The Document: Declaration of Feminism* was published calling for a "feminist-socialist revolution," saying:

> We must go back to matriarchies . . . to ancient female religions [like witchcraft]. . . . In order to break the tyranny of class oppression, it is necessary to establish a socialist order. . . . In the final hours of capitalism we will dance on the grave of corporate America. . . . Marriage is the key institution that has failed us and we must work to destroy it. . . . The nuclear family must be replaced with a new form of family where individuals live and work together to help meet the needs of all people in the society. . . . With the destruction of the nuclear family must come a new way of looking at children. They must be seen as the responsibility of an *entire society* rather than individual parents.

It was the time of "women's liberation," and John D. Rockefeller III (founder of the Population Council in 1952) in his 1973 book *The Second American Revolution* applauded sexual liberation and the "humanistic revolution," while disparaging "old-fashioned nationalism." The *Roe v. Wade* and *Doe v. Bolton* Supreme Court decisions were also handed down in 1973 indicating that abortion is entirely a woman's decision with the father having no control over this killing of his child. With feminists and the government thus declaring fathers irrelevant in this fundamental decision, one must wonder how leftists today can be surprised that the numbers of fathers who have deserted their families has grown since 1973.

Four years later, Mary Jo Bane would be quoted in an Associated Press story in the *Tulsa Sunday World* (August 21, 1977) as stating: "We really don't know how to raise children. If we want to talk about equality of opportunity for children, then the fact that children are raised in families means there's no equality. It's a dilemma. In order to raise children with equality, we must take them away from families and communally raise them."

About this same time, HEW executive assistant Eddie Bernice Johnson (who would later become a member of Congress from Texas) advocated the licensing of parents before they would be permitted to have children, saying: "We require almost every endeavor or profession to be licensed—why not the single most important responsibility which a parent can ever have?"

Not long thereafter, Prof. Gene Stephens of the College of Criminal Justice at the University of South Carolina wrote in "Crime in the Year 2000" (*The Futurist,* April 1981):

> Parental care in the year 2000 may be different from today's and better, since by then the movement to license or certify parents may be well under way. In most cases, certified couples would be allowed to have their own natural children. In some instances, however, genetic scanning may find that some women and men can produce "super" babies but are not well suited to rear them.... Child breeding and rearing, then, may be considered too important to be left to chance.... Man's ability to control his fellow man will surely grow greater, not less, over the next two decades.

And in 1994, Jack Westman's *Licensing Parents* was published and is being sold at the World Future Society Bookstore.

Lest one think the administration of President Clinton would be friendly to families, on April 21, 1997, President Clinton signed Executive Order 13045, which among other things revoked President Ronald Reagan's Executive Order 12606 (September 2, 1987). The executive order by President Reagan said in part:

> In formulating and implementing policies and regulations that may have significant impact on family formation, maintenance, and general well-being, Executive Departments and agencies should, to the extent permitted by law, assess such measures in light of the following questions: (a) Does this action by government strengthen or erode the stability of the family and, particularly, the marital commitment? (b) Does this action strengthen or erode the authority and rights of parents in the education, nurture, and supervision of their children?

During the presidency of Bill Clinton, Mary Jo Bane for several years would be an assistant secretary at the Department of Health and Human Services. This isn't surprising, given the fact that four years before Bane's quote above, Hillary Rodham (who would be Bill Clinton's wife) wrote in the *Harvard Educational Review* (November 1973) of her rejection of "the belief that families are private, non-political units whose interests subsume those of children."

In this same year of 1973, *The New Socialist Revolution* by Michael Lerner (who would be an important adviser to First Lady Hillary Rodham Clinton) was published, in which he proclaimed:

> Education will be radically transformed in our socialist community. . . . There will be no grading, but comprehensive reports on each youngster's development. A key element will be helping young people learn how to work and act together. . . . Particularly in the elementary school . . . the main emphasis will be on learning how to . . . live and work collectively. . . . The next level is learning some series of skills, for one's first set of jobs, and this learning will be repeated periodically as jobs are rotated. . . . After the socialist revolution, education will have a much broader role. . . . Education will become a permanent feature of life, not limited to the youthful period. . . .

Doesn't this sound like the cooperative learning, outcome-based skills, no grade levels, lifelong learning, etc. being promoted today? And won't "education as a permanent feature of life" (lifelong learning) be used as an excuse to monitor everyone constantly from cradle to grave? Actually, government monitoring and control could begin *before* the cradle, as educational leader David Hornbeck (who has been chairman of the Carnegie Foundation for the Advancement of Teaching, and later became superintendent of Philadelphia Public Schools) in his co-edited *Human Capital and America's Future* (1991) would propose that the government's duty "would begin during a mother's pregnancy." In an approach he admits may be subject to the charge of "big brotherism," Hornbeck proposes legislation creating a "State Board for Children and Families (BCF)" which would have

> a new affirmative duty for government to assure the health and non-academic well-being of each child until age 18 or graduation from high school, whichever comes first. . . . There may be some areas of child need in which the family will play the dominant role—before school and breakfast, for example. In others, such as after school support, the BCF may play the central role. The board would have the

responsibility to work with the family to sort out the balance of roles. . . . Court orders and/or legislation must be our primary vehicles to provoke and sustain the magnitude and kind of change that is necessary. . . . Success must not be left to chance. Responsibility must be fixed. All of this must be done legislatively.

(Also see *Full Service Schools: A Revolution in Health and Social Services for Children, Youth and Families* by Joy Dryfoos, supported by the Carnegie Corporation, published in 1994.)

The year after Hornbeck's book was published, Bill Clinton was elected president. Almost immediately after the election, the president of Carnegie's National Center on Education and the Economy (NCEE), Marc Tucker, wrote a letter to Hillary Clinton on November 11, 1992, stating:

I still cannot believe you won. But utter delight that you did pervades all the circles in which I move. I met last Wednesday in David Rockefeller's office with him. . . . It was a great celebration. . . . The subject we were discussing was what you and Bill should now do about education, training and labor market policy. Following that meeting, I chaired another in Washington on the same topic. Those present at the second meeting included David Hornbeck, Lauren Resnick. . . . Ira Magaziner was also invited to this meeting. Our purpose in these meetings was to propose concrete actions that the Clinton administration could take. . . . We took a very large leap forward in terms of how to advance the agenda on which you and we have all been working—a practical plan for putting all of the major components of the system in place within four years, by the time Bill has to run again. . . . We think the great opportunity you have is to remold the entire American system for human resources development. . . . What is essential is that we create a seamless web of opportunities to develop one's skills that literally extends from cradle to grave and is the same system for everyone. It needs to be a system . . . guided by clear standards that define the stages of the system for the people who progress through it and regulated on the basis of outcomes. . . . To implement this vision . . . use your proposal for an apprenticeship system as the keystone of a strategy for putting the whole new post-secondary training system in place . . . the whole new human resources system nationwide over the next four years, using the [renamed] apprenticeship idea as the entering wedge.... Create one national system.... [Criteria for selection includes] commitment to developing an outcome- and performance-based system for human resources development system.... [Program components include] develop uniform reporting system for providers, requiring them to provide information in that format on characteristics of clients. Develop computer-based system for combining this data at local labor market board offices with employment data from the state ... including subsequent employment histories for graduates. Design all programs around the forthcoming general education standards.... We propose that Bill take a leaf out of the German book. One of the most important reasons that large German employers offer apprenticeship slots to German youngsters is that they fear, with good reason, that if they don't volunteer to do so, the law will require it. Bill could ... do the same.... Radical changes in attitudes, values and beliefs are required to move any combination of these agendas.

Many elements of the NCEE proposals were incorporated into H.R. 1617 ("The Careers Act") passed by the U.S. House of Representatives in September 1995. Not only do some aspects of the aforementioned proposals resemble the Soviet Polytechnical Education System, but there are even broader implications involving the U.N. All of these "school-to-work" programs fit neatly into an international effort to control people (e.g., whether they may be aborted, what education they receive, what jobs they have, etc.). At about the same time the U.N. was holding its "population (control) and development" conference in Cairo (where Third World countries were financially pressured to go along with the "Programme of Action" or not have their loans renewed, etc.), the U.N.'s *Human Development Report, 1994* was published, including "An Agenda for the Social Summit" in Copenhagen, March 1995. Not only did the final draft document of the "Programme of Action" going into Copenhagen sound similar in one way to NCEE's proposed "human resources development system" and to H.R. 1617 when it listed as an objective "to establish the creation of productive employment as a central objective ... and to reinforce international cooperation to that effect," but the *Human Development Report, 1994* included the following objectives: (1) a global tax, (2) strengthening the U.N. militarily while closing nations' military bases and reducing their military spending, and (3) a "Social Charter" pledging "a new global civil society" based upon "global" governance. And the *Report's* "suggested" "Social Charter" included: "We strongly believe that the United Nations must become the principal custodian of our global human security. Towards this end, we are determined to strengthen the development role of the United Nations and to give it wide-ranging decision-making powers in the socio-economic field by establishing an Economic Security Council" (with no nation having a veto). Therefore, what we are facing is not simply a "planned" future at the national level, but also at the international level under the U.N.

Dr. Felix Wittmer warned about the shift in education from the individual to the collective or "groupthink" in his *Conquest of the American Mind* (1956), in which he wrote:

> Have you ever read a book on "curriculum development"? . . . As the years went by, and your children passed through the grades, you may have noticed that a change was going on. Subject matter, teaching methods, types of study, everything changed. If you put two and two together, you realized that the emphasis shifted from the individual to the group. . . . Competition, it seems, has become old hat. "Attitudes" and "group relationships" were the thing.

The type of education children were receiving was becoming humanistic, but the global planners realized that to shape the values of youth to accept world socialism, they could not wait until children entered the public schools. They had to be reached at an earlier age, and that meant separating pre-school youth from their parents. But how could that be accomplished? A hypothetical scenario could have gone something like this. Living standards would rise dramatically between the end of World War II and the early 1970s. Then a period of rising inflation would occur (through a manufactured oil crisis, etc.), so that both spouses would have to enter the workforce just to maintain their standard of living. This would mean having to put their children into (government licensed) day care, and the rising feminist movement made this acceptable to many women. Traditional women, however, would still choose to remain home and rear their own children, so laws would need to be passed granting social service workers immunity from liability if they seized children from homes simply on the basis of alleged abuse or even "emotional neglect" (whatever that means).

Alger Hiss (who would be selected president of the Carnegie Endowment for International Peace in December 1946, and on January 25, 1950, would be sentenced to five years in prison for perjury after having denied that he was engaged in espionage for the Soviet Union) had in July 1946 persuaded the founders of the World Health Organization (WHO) to include in their constitution the following broad definition of "health"—"Health is a state of complete physical, mental, and social well-being" ("social" or group "well-being" is one of the justifications for socialism). Hiss' close friend Brock Chisholm (1959 Humanist of the Year) became head of WHO, and in the February 1946 issue of *Psychiatry* had written that to achieve world government, it is necessary to remove from the minds of men their individualism, loyalty to family tradition, national patriotism, and religious dogmas. He further stated:

> We have swallowed all manner of poisonous certainties fed us by our parents, our Sunday and day school teachers, our politicians, our priests. . . . The reinterpretation and eventual eradication of the concept of right and wrong which has been the basis of child training, the substitution of intelligent and rational thinking for faith in the certainties of old people, these are the belated objectives. . . for charting the necessary changes in human behavior.

This was followed by the permissive child-rearing theories of Dr. Benjamin Spock in the 1950s, followed by the "me" generation of the 1960s. Public schools facilitated the student as autonomous moral decision-maker by teaching students situation ethics via values clarification techniques. This in part led to the widespread "don't impose your morality on me" philosophy of the 1970s, which the public schools reinforced into the 1980s with "critical thinking," which often turned out to be lessons in criticizing authority (e.g., parents, clergy, and other adults). Then the 1987 edition of the *Diagnostic and Statistical Manual of Mental Disorders* (characterized as "the bible" of the mental health professions) described the symptoms of "Oppositional Defiant Disorder" as: "Children with this disorder commonly are argumentative with adults, frequently lose their tempers, swear and are often angry, resentful and easily annoyed by others. They frequently actively defy adult requests and rules. . . ." With this definition, it is easy to see how nearly every child in the U.S. could be labeled "at risk" by health and social service workers. Then based upon the promulgation of the "it takes a whole village to raise a child" (or Paideia) philosophy, social engineers will claim "government intervention" in family life is required, and socialism will be here.

Remember that socialism emphasizes society or the community or the larger group over the individual or any individual family. William Shirer in *The Rise and Fall of the Third Reich* (1960) explained that the "Hitler Youth" organization indoctrinated children in the Nazi (National Socialist) philosophy, and parents withholding youth from that organization could have their children taken away by the State. Nazi minister of the interior, Dr. Wilhelm Frick, declared: "The period in which the task of the school was considered to be to develop the individual is past. The new school proceeds on principle from the idea of the community, which is the age-old legacy of our Germanic ancestors."

Does this sound like some social service workers and "outcome-based education" (OBE) in the U.S. today? And relevant to school-to-work along with lifelong-learning portfolios in the U.S. today is the following quote from Shirer's book:

> [The Workbook was introduced] and eventually no worker could be hired unless he possessed one. In it was kept a record of his skills and employment. The workbook not only provided the State and the employer with up-to-date data on every single employee in the nation but was used to tie a worker to the bench. If he desired to leave for other employment his employer could retain his workbook, which meant that he could not be legally employed elsewhere. . . .

Will students without "skill certificates" be unable to get jobs in the future?

Group learning, called "cooperative learning," is a key ingredient in OBE, and while most people believe that OBE is a relatively recent educational concept, in 1938 the National Education Association (NEA) published *The Purposes of Education in American Democracy,* in which was written: "Measurement of outcomes must be directly related to the objectives." The publication also stated that

> education has, on the whole, been altogether too much concerned with facts, and too little concerned with values. . . . There should be a much greater concern with the development of attitudes, interests, ideals and habits. . . . Our schools should

give prizes not to the one who wins more credit for himself, but to the one who cooperates most effectively with others. . . . The educated citizen is a cooperating member of the world community.

The NEA has long advocated world government, and in this publication, "world citizenship" is listed as an objective of civic responsibility. Other key terms in the current educational reform movement are public accountability, partnerships, learning work skills and tolerance, and lifelong learning. In the 1938 NEA publication, one reads:

> Efforts to take the public into account must be supplemented by efforts to take the public into confidence and, finally, into partnership. . . . Are students becoming more skillful in doing some type of useful work? . . . Are they acquiring skills? . . . Are they learning to be fair and tolerant in situations where conflicts arise? . . . Education is not gained in a few years in school; it is a lifetime enterprise. . . .

Almost fifty years later, Utah Superintendent of Public Instruction Leland Burningham on July 27, 1984, wrote a letter to U.S. Secretary of Education Terrel Bell saying:

> I am forwarding this letter to accompany the proposal which you recommended Bill Spady [father of OBE] and I prepare in connection with Outcome-Based Education. This proposal centers around the detailed process by which we will work together to implement OBE. . . . This will make it possible to put OBE in place, not only in Utah but in all schools of the nation.

OBE includes such things as values or character education, the role of John Dewey's humanistic psychology, wholistic education including social experience, "guided discovery," cooperative learning, and "learning to learn" emphasized over content. Is it just coincidence that *all* of these are described in a 1984 UNESCO publication *The Theory of Curriculum Content in the USSR*? Remember what Ford Foundation president H. Rowan Gaither said earlier about "a comfortable merger with the Soviet Union," and is it also a coincidence that Terrel Bell received his doctorate as a Ford Foundation fellow a few years after Gaither's remark?

Relevant to the "me" generation who were taught there are no moral absolutes, and today's OBE "study groups" training students to be workers (school-to-work) who "get along with others," the following is foreign correspondent Edward Hunter's testimony in the *Congressional Record* (March 13, 1958):

> If the prisoner [of the communists] was the quite usual type we had been developing, who had been brought up just to ask, "What's in it for me?" he was considered a fine prospect [for brainwashing]. . . . I have been watching developments under communism in other parts of the world, and now I see exactly the same developments here in America . . . the penetration of our leadership circles by a softening up . . . [the] penetration of our educational circles by a similar state of mind . . . the liquidation of our attitudes on what we used to recognize as right and wrong, and what we need to accept as absolute moral standards . . . [teaching] that everything changes, and that what is right or wrong, good or bad, changes as well. . . . What they do say to the rest of us is to be objective; and then they twist that word "objective" into what they mean by dialectical materialism. . . . The same "discussion meetings" [or "study groups"] that were held in the schools and factories of Red China, I now read about in these diaries [of slain Chinese guerrilla fighters]. . . . Today [in the U.S.] personnel departments ask if the man "gets along" with everybody. They do not ask what is his individuality; they ask how he conforms. When we raise a young man to believe that at all costs he must get on with everyone, we have put him into a state of mind that guarantees, if he falls into the hands of an enemy . . . that he will react as he had been raised, to try "to get on." . . . [The communists'] objective is to make the same use of the American people as they make of the Czechs in the uranium mines of Czechoslovakia, and as they make of the Chinese in the mills of China. We are to become subjects of a "new world order." . . .

With much of the current educational reform emphasizing "school-to-work skills," it is interesting to note that in Vladimir Turchenko's *The Scientific and Technological Revolution and the Revolution in Education* (1976, and imported into the U.S.), he describes Soviet education as including "instruction from a younger age, linking instruction with productive labor, 'continuous' education. . . . Under socialism, education has become not only the personal affair of every individual, but also a concern of society as a whole" (sounds like the slogan, "it takes a whole village to raise a child").

It is also interesting to note in Eugene Maxwell Boyce's *The Coming Revolution in Education* (1983) that this professor of educational administration at the University of Georgia declared:

> In the Communist ideology the function of universal education is clear, and easily understood. . . . Education is tied directly to jobs—control of the job being the critical control point in an authoritarian state. Level of education, and consequently the level of employment, is determined first, by level of achievement in school. They do not educate people for jobs that do not exist. No such direct, controlled, relationship between education and jobs exists in democratic countries.

In the same year (1983), national OBE consultant Howard Gardner's *Frames of Mind: The Theory of Multiple Intelligences* (including an acknowledgment to the Carnegie Corporation) was published, with Gardner proposing: "Individual profiles must be considered in light of goals pursued by the wider society; and sometimes, in fact, individuals with gifts in certain directions must nonetheless be guided along other, less favored paths, simply because the needs of the culture are particularly urgent in that realm at that time."

Four years later, Lawrence Feinberg in the *Washington Post* (August 17, 1987) would report that David Harman (Columbia University Teachers College) and Thomas Sticht (who has conducted major research on reading for the U.S. Army and the Ford Foundation) said what may be crucial in the U.S. is the dependability of a labor force and how well it can be managed and trained, not its general educational level—although a small cadre of highly educated, creative people is essential to growth. Feinberg also reported both researchers as indicating that changing values, among other things, are probably more important than reading, in moving low-income families into the middle class.

The changing of moral values had begun in earnest in the 1950s when Benjamin Bloom *et al.* wrote in *Taxonomy of Educational Objectives, Handbook I: Cognitive Domain* (1956) that "we recognize the point of view that truth and knowledge are only relative and that there are no hard and fast truths which exist for all time and all places."

Two years later, Ronald Lippett *et al.* wrote *The Dynamics of Planned Change* (1958) "stimulated by the ideas and example of Kurt Lewin." Lewin had helped found the National Training Laboratories in 1947, and wrote in the journal *Human Relations* in that year that "successful change includes unfreezing, moving [to the new level], and (re)freezing group life on the new level." Lippett *et al.* would write about the "moving" phase in terms of (values) "clarification" and "transformation," and explain that some change agents "feel that the process of change itself will determine the goal and lead the client to it." They then described "interdependence as a factor in the change process" and spoke of "achieving terminal relationship" and said "ways of handling conflict between opposed loyalties are an important part of the change process." (These last three quotes will be significant in considering the interdependence established by GATT and the World Trade Organization, the difficulty in withdrawing from them, and the opposing loyalties of globalists and patriotic nationalists.)

Strategies for accomplishing "change" were exposed by Jo Hindman in her December 15, 1958, *Human Events* article regarding "social engineering," in which she quoted Dr. Harry A. Overstreet in his *The Great Enterprise* (1952) as saying: "A man may be angrily against technical aid to backward countries . . . and the preaching of social rather than salvational religion. . . . Such people may appear 'normal' . . . but they are well along the road to mental illness." The message is that "mentally ill" people must "change." But how? Hindman described the process of "group dynamics" in education, for example, "whereby committees studying various educational subjects were manipulated into coming up with predetermined conclusions" (e.g., favoring federal aid). She related also the New Deal "Centerville" project where "American families were arranged in a neighborhood according to a chart laid out upon social engineering principles. A 'key' family was strategically located so that its influence would have far-reaching effects in molding the attitudes of the entire community." She then exposed the technique of obtaining "canned" samples of public opinion, using the example of a 1957 State Department poll "engineered" to obtain foreign aid, stating: "Inspection of the State Department poll discloses a striking resemblance to one detail of sociometry's (J. L. Moreno's *Sociometry: An Approach to a New Political Orientation*) political program, which calls for a Federal Department of Human Relations, tied to miniature substructures rooted in school, home and workshop." Hindman explained that "the files in school offices, containing cumulative information concerning pupils and their parents, provide information from which sociometrists perform research, write papers, and publish social engineering conclusions." And she mentioned the "guided minds" program in the public schools as "a subdivision of the 'social engineering' movement."

Three years later, Warren Bennis, Kenneth Benne, and Robert Chin (all have been associated with the National Training Laboratories) edited *The Planning of Change* (1961) and credited Kurt Lewin's work. The editors declared that they are "living in an age whose single constant is radical change." And under Part 2 (of the book) which is titled "Conceptual Tools for the Change-Agent," Robert Gunderson referred to "facilitators, harmonizers," etc. and stated that "the world community is their workshop." Kurt Lewin and Paul Grabbe in their chapter titled "Principles of Re-Education," pronounced that "the re-educative process changes the individual's [or group's] *cognitive* structure . . . including all his facts, concepts, beliefs, and expectations. It modifies his *valences and values*." And the last section of their chapter was titled "Creation of an In-Group and the Acceptance of a New Value System," where an "In-Group" is described as "a group in which the membership feel belongingness" (youth will want to be accepted by the "in-crowd," and will therefore accept their values).

More recently, *Spiral Dynamics: Mastering Values, Complexity and Change* (1993, revised 1996) by Don Beck and Christopher Cowan of the National Values Center (Santa Barbara, California) describes how individuals, organizations, and societies can be changed (including innovations in working, education, health care, religion, and politics) by meshing chaos theory, quantum physics, contemporary brain research, and general systems theory.

Bloom *et al.* in 1964 wrote *Taxonomy of Educational Objectives, Handbook II,*

Affective Domain, further stating that "a large part of what we call 'good teaching' is the teacher's ability to attain affective objectives through challenging the students' fixed beliefs," and offering "illustrative objectives" such as "judges problems and issues in terms of situations, issues, purposes, and consequences involved rather than in terms of fixed, dogmatic precepts or emotionally wishful thinking."

The authors continue:

> the evidence collected so far suggests that a single hour of classroom activity under certain conditions may bring about a major reorganization in . . . affective behaviors. The affective domain is, in retrospect, a virtual "Pandora's Box." . . . We are not entirely sure that opening our "box" is necessarily a good thing; we are certain that it is not likely to be a source of peace and harmony among the members of a school staff. . . . It is in this "box" that the most influential controls are to be found. The affective domain contains the forces that determine the nature of an individual's life and ultimately the life of an entire people.

The "affective domain" would also be the point of attack against Christians via encounter groups, as Dr. William Schutz writing in *Redbook* (July 1968) revealed: "When a Christian organization like the YMCA puts its boys through an encounter group to develop their independence, they may find some of the boys questioning Christian principles. These are not only possibilities, they happen, but they are necessary risks for individual development."

Schutz's comments are important because he was director of Esalen Institute's resident program at Big Sur, California. Esalen is where Fritz Perl's gestalt therapy was emphasized with "guided daydreams" that were described as a form of hypnosis. Esalen would later engage in "hot tub" diplomacy, inviting many officials from the Soviet Union to "experience" their offerings. They would sponsor Boris Yeltsin's trip to the U.S. before he would become Russian leader; and the executive director of the Esalen Institute in 1989, Jim Garrison (who would name the Christic Institute), would later be the president of the Gorbachev Foundation/USA which would locate at the Presidio (formerly a prestigious American military base in San Francisco) in 1992, and which would have as its purpose "to affirm the spirit of Gorbachev's vision of a new world order . . . and apply his vision on a global level."

In an article, "One World, Under Gorby" (*San Francisco Weekly,* May 31–June 6, 1995), Garrison stated:

> Over the next 20 to 30 years, we are going to end up with world government. It's inevitable.... You are going to see more Yugoslavias ... but in and through this turbulence is the recognition that we have to empower the United Nations and that we have to govern and regulate human interaction.... There's going to be conflict, coercion and consensus. That's all part of what will be required as we give birth to the first global civilization.

In 1992, Bill Clinton was elected president, and for many years had attended a sort of "Esalen East" called "Renaissance Weekend," which was referred to by the *New York Times* as a "New Age Retreat." *Newsweek* also described Bill Clinton as the first "New Age President."

Returning briefly to the 1960s, the National Institute of Mental Health granted psychologist B. F. Skinner $283,000 on February 18, 1964 (Grant K6-MH 21755) to be paid over a ten-year period to write *Beyond Freedom and Dignity.* Skinner had already written *Walden II* (1948) about a utopian society based upon the scientific control of human behavior, where children would be raised in communal nurseries, and theology and history would be suppressed. In *Beyond Freedom and Dignity* (1971), Skinner (the inventor of "the teaching machine" and "the father of programmed instruction") maintained that the concepts of freedom and dignity must be discarded, and that human behavior be conditioned by an elite. Not long after *Beyond Freedom and Dignity* was published, Rep. Cornelius Gallagher (NJ) told the U.S. House of Representatives in a speech titled "Skinnering the Taxpayers":

> We disclosed in 1970 that at least 250,000 American grammar school children are receiving behavioral modification drugs, most often the amphetamines or "speed" as they are commonly called. The committee report released in 1968 entitled "Privacy and the National Data Bank Concept" based on the computer hearings was called "a gem" by computer specialists and on the floor of the other body, Senator Sam Ervin referred to it as "a concise classic." ... In July 1971, the distinguished expert of Soviet affairs, Victor Zorza, described the growth of massive computerized

information systems in Russia. He describes the manner in which the planners of the Soviet computerized systems intend to use it as a weapon of thought control. Zorza writes: "But the main purpose of any such system would be to prevent any disloyal ideas from even taking shape in the heads of Soviet citizens . . . the full records of his psychological characteristics and actions could be used to devise an approach that would quickly persuade him . . . that his best interests require him to conform to the political guidance of his spiritual advisor at the KGB." What better description of Skinner's "technology of behavior"?

To see how the computer might be used in the future, read the U.S. Department of Education's 1967 publication *OE 100,* which stands for the 100th anniversary of the federal Office of Education in that year. Toward the end of the document is a story titled "1997," in which one reads:

> Johnny Brooks, eight years old, is a student in Iowa Public Education Concenter 417. To his parents' consternation, Johnny's "classes" at Concenter 417 consist only of him. The pupils frequently do gather in groups, for seminar-like discussions. . . . The learning console at which Johnny spends much of his time in Concenter 417 appears to be an enclosed desk with a television set and a typewriter built into it. He starts his lesson by inserting his aluminum identification plate into the console demand slot. . . . His console and concenter—like all the other concenters around the Davenport metropolitan area—are connected to the Educational Resources Center downtown. There, the record of Johnny's progress that has been tabulated by computers is combed by a team of psychologists, programmers, expert teachers of everything from arithmetic to zoology, remedial specialists, and guidance counselors. Neither Johnny nor anyone else knows what grade he's in. . . . He proceeds at his own pace. . . . In Johnny's world, education never stops; learning is a year-round, life-long process.

That this story was titled "1997" seems to be right on target. After all, by May 1984 Dustin Heuston of Utah's World Institute for Computer-Assisted Teaching (WICAT) said in "Discussion—Developing the Potential of an Amazing Tool" (*Schooling and Technology, vol.3, Planning for the Future: A Collaborative Model*):

"We've been absolutely staggered by realizing that the computer has the capability to act as if it were ten of the top psychologists working with one student. . . . Won't it be wonderful when . . . no one can get between that child and that curriculum?"

Predictions regarding socialism, along with its threat, have been made by educators and in the field of education for many years. In Alexis de Tocqueville's *Democracy in America* in 1840 (translated later by George Lawrence), he remarks concerning potential despotisms that "I do not expect their leaders to be tyrants, but rather schoolmasters."

And in the original Henry Reeve translation, de Tocqueville further explains:

> Above this race of men stands an immense and tutelary power, which takes upon itself alone to secure their gratifications and to watch over their fate. . . . After having thus successively taken each member of the community in its powerful grasp and fashioned him at will, the supreme power then extends its arm over the whole community. . . . The will of man is not shattered, but softened, bent, and guided. . . . It does not tyrannize, but it compresses, enervates, extinguishes, and stupefies a people, till each nation is reduced to nothing better than a flock of timid and industrious animals, of which the government is the shepherd.

In the December 21, 1954 *New York World-Telegram and Sun,* John Temple Graves offered a similar warning concerning the subtleness of socialism, including its effect upon "progressive educators," saying:

> A greater killer has been socialism. Not Communism, but its pale sister who doesn't know the facts of life—socialism. The socialism . . . which forgets ethics and the individual for the state. The socialism which gives us social-minded preachers who neglect God and men for "society." The socialism which persuaded so-called progressive educators to forget education for mere vocation and group-mindedness, and to propose liberty for babies even as a social-minded state created slavery for grown-ups. This socialism is a far greater home menace than out-and-out communism, for it is respectable, legal, not capable of being jailed or deported by the FBI or hounded down by Congressional committees.

Twenty-one years later, the *Journal of Teacher Education* (Fall 1975) published "Humanizing Teacher Education for the Last Quarter of the Twentieth Century" by Edward Durchame and Robert Nash, who believed teachers of the future will be called "human service educators . . . developing an ideology of humanistic socialism . . . training in the politics of power; the phenomenology of the change agent; ethical ways of dislodging or supporting those in power . . . and the practical [and moral] strategies necessary for attaining positions of power and influence."

This was the year after Theodore Brameld wrote *The Teacher as World Citizen* (1974) commemorating Edward Bellamy's *Looking Backward* and also using the term "humanistic socialism." Bellamy's book, published in 1888, looks backward from A.D. 2000 describing how a "socialist utopia" came into being in America, where money had come to be replaced by cards with credit on them, where students would perform three years of menial service, where crime would be treated as just a mental disease, and where a woman selected by the women of the U.S. could veto any legislation regarding the rights of women. The date given at the beginning of the book by leading collectivist educator Brameld is December 26, 2000, and looking backward, he relates (actually writing this in 1974) that the World Community of Nations (WCN) began in 1990 (curiously, the same year President Bush announced "the new world order") as a transnational government with a World Order Party based on the ideals of "humanistic socialism," and children are reared from the nursery through high school under the auspices of a World Education Authority. Similarly in *And Madly Teach* (1949) author Mortimer Smith wrote:

> Let us imagine the life of an average American in the year 2000.... Private schools by then will have been abolished as anti-social, and the child will perforce go to a public school ... preparing him "for the realization of his best self in the higher loyalty" of serving the state.... The state is supreme.... [In the future] the school building is used all day for youth and all evening for adults.... Our schools under the political power [will] have aggregated unto themselves more and more functions. ... If there is any unity in our discordant world of today it consists in a devotion to this socialistic principle,

of which Smith disapproved and tried to warn Americans.

Perhaps the main problem parents face today concerning the education of youth is that they do not know what is going on at schools regarding their children. For example, the Georgia Department of Education produced a document titled "Psychological Education" containing a "Group Contract" for students to sign which indicated the students would not tell anyone (including parents) what happened in the groups without the groups' permission. And in May 1995, the Early Childhood Developmental Enrichment Center in Illinois (and funded by the Illinois State Board of Education) sent questionnaires to some teachers regarding a number of students with the instructions: "Please be sure not to send this form home to parents."

One way parents can at least stop the indoctrination of their children with secular humanism in the public schools would be to have school boards pass resolutions (or legislatures pass laws) stating that if Judeo-Christian values cannot be explicitly taught as such in the public schools, then no other values can either (e.g., humanistic values in sex education) because that would be discrimination. Perhaps since the Ten Commandments have been removed from schools and other public properties, resolutions and laws can also be passed to remove pagan deities from public properties around the U.S. (Demeter in Annapolis, Minerva on the California state seal, Ceres on Vermont's capitol, etc.).

In terms of legislation today, children are being nationalized via "Goals 2000," which had national and community service requirements as well as such home-intervention programs as "Parents As Teachers." Years ago (1793), William Godwin warned against the nationalization of education when he wrote *An Enquiry Concerning Political Justice, and Its Influence on General Virtue and Happiness,* in which he declared, "The project of a national education ought uniformly to be discouraged, on account of its obvious alliance with national government."

And when Dwight Eisenhower was president of Columbia University (1948–1952), he warned that federal aid to education was "another vehicle by which the believers in paternalism, if not outright socialism, will gain still additional power for the central government."

Also regarding the nationalization of education, *Richmond Times-Dispatch* editorial page editor Robert Holland on October 6, 1994, wrote to U.S. Secretary of Education Richard Riley regarding "Goals 2000":

> I have today obtained a copy of the "Community Action Toolkit" of the National Education Goals Panel, of which you are a member.... The kit makes this statement: "Only by changing the attitudes and behaviors of community members will it be possible to reach the National Education Goals." With all due respect, sir, that does not sound like the government believes that we citizens have any choice regarding the shape education reform will take. In fact, isn't such a government-directed propaganda campaign unprecedented in America's history? Some of the topics in this kit: Describe Allies and Opponents. Identify Change Agents. Trouble-shooting in the event of opposition. And avoid the term Outcome-Based Education.... Finally, sir, what is your authority under the United States Constitution to conduct a campaign aimed at rigging the outcomes of the education debate in every local community in America?

In *Education Week* (April 6, 1994), Stephen Arons (professor of legal studies at the University of Massachusetts) said about "Goals 2000" that it "will lead to the creation of a national curriculum ... [and] the political and bureaucratic specification of official knowledge." And in *Education Week* (September 7, 1994), Kenneth Goodman (past president of the International Reading Association) exclaimed concerning "the Reagan-Bush-Clinton educational reforms" regarding standards:

> I accuse the politicians and technicians of the standards movement of using
> standards as a cover for a well-orchestrated attempt to centralize power and thus
> control who will teach, who will learn, what will be taught in the nation's schools,
> and who will determine the curriculum for schools and for teacher education. . . .
> The standards movement promises the political power brokers that by controlling
> outcomes they can control schools while appearing to support local control.

In Arthur Schlesinger, Jr.'s *Partisan Review* article quoted earlier, he referred to "a secret long known to the British who, as D. W. Brogan has put it, 'change anything except the appearance of things.'"

Another piece of legislation furthering the nationalization of education was HR 6 (reauthorization of the Elementary and Secondary Education Act), which was passed by Congress and signed by President Clinton. As with "Goals 2000," a great deal of federal money was dangled in front of the states to cause them "voluntarily" to accept this ESEA legislation. Most states wanted the money, and therefore accepted the "national standards" (based on the "national goals") that went with it. To meet these standards, most states will develop new statewide subjective (OBE) assessments. Even if these are not mandated for *every* child initially, states' accreditation and certification requirements will soon impact private school and home school students (e.g. college admissions or obtaining a job will be impossible without a "Certificate of Initial Mastery" which will be obtainable only by doing well on the new statewide subjective OBE assessments), who will be at a distinct disadvantage if they have not been educated to meet these assessments. This could mean the death of traditional private school and home school education as we know it today.

Regarding the "national goals," measurements can be extremely privacy–invading, as vol. 108, supplement 1, 1993, of *Public Health Reports* by the U.S. Public Health Service contains "Youth Risk Behavior Surveillance System Questions to Measure National Education Goal 6," which includes questions like "How many times have you used marijuana?" and "Have you ever had sexual intercourse?" And in the "national standards" released for U.S. History, there was no mention of people like Paul Revere, Thomas Edison, and the Wright brothers, because as the co–director (Gary Nash) of the commission putting together the standards proclaimed, the traditional "emphasis on dates, facts, places, events" was something he wanted to "bury." This, of course, means that what little traditional education students were receiving will be even further diminished. Perhaps that is why the Association for Supervision and Curriculum Development released its 1994–1995 "Professional Liability Protection Plan for Educators," which stated that with the plan,

> you will be protected against a broad range of exposures, including the following allegations (whether those allegations are true or false): . . . failure to educate; improper methods employed in instruction, counseling, research design, etc.; negative consequences in the implementation of the recommendations of research studies; hiring unqualified persons. . . .

Once education has been nationalized, then it can be internationalized along the lines desired by UNESCO, as stated by its first director-general, Sir Julian Huxley (1962 Humanist of the Year), in *UNESCO: Its Purpose and Its Philosophy* (1948) where he declared: "In its education program [UNESCO] can stress the ultimate need for world political unity and familiarize all peoples with the implications of the transfer of full sovereignty from separate nations to a world organization. . . . Political unification in some sort of world government will be required."

Later, former U.S. Senator William Benton, speaking to UNESCO, would say: "We are at the beginning of a long process of breaking down the walls of our national sovereignty. In this, UNESCO can be, and indeed must be, the pioneer." (See the September 4, 1962, "Extension of Remarks" by Congressman James Utt in the *Congressional Record*.)

Education can also be internationalized along the lines proposed by the U.S. Coalition for Education for All (USCEA), an outgrowth of the World Conference on Education for All, which was sponsored by, among others, the World Bank, UNESCO, UNICEF, and the U.N. Development Program (UNDP). The UNDP funds Third World abortions and was headed by Rhodes Scholar James Speth, who was a senior advisor to President-elect Clinton's transition team. In USCEA's mailing, "World Citizenship: A Global Ethic for Sustainable Development" (by the Baha'i International Community, that from its beginning about 150 years ago has advocated a "common faith" and a world government), it states that in shaping values, attitudes and behaviors, "world citizenship (a universal principle) should be a part of the standard education of every child."

Furthermore, the Boy Scouts of America have as part of its merit badge series "Citizenship in the World" promoting world citizenship, the U.N., the World Court, the World Federalist Association (leading organization working for world federal government), and the General Agreement on Tariffs and Trade (GATT). That GATT is among the things being promoted by the Boy Scouts organization is important because the advocates of a world socialist government believe that a one-world economy is a necessary step in securing their ultimate goal (see pages 117–118 this book quoting Sen. Malone). GATT began in 1947, and regarding the latest round (the Uruguay Round) of the GATT negotiations, even liberal Harvard University law professor Lawrence Tribe has said it "would entail a significant shift of sovereignty from state and local governments to the World Trade Organization (WTO)."

European Parliament member Sir James Goldsmith's book, *The Trap* (1994), is also severely critical of GATT. And in his testimony November 15, 1994, to the Senate Commerce Committee, he said:

> What we are witnessing is the divorce of the interests of the major corporations and the interests of society as a whole.... We have a system being proposed which will result in massive unemployment, massive hemorrhaging of jobs and capital, but which will increase Corporate profits.... There is absolutely no doubt whatsoever that the World Trade Organization is a major diminution of sovereignty. ... GATT, global free trade, is the replacement utopia for Marxism. It's another one of these mad utopias."

The April 17, 1995, national news announcement that our nation's food surplus was being reduced to comply with GATT also reveals the possibility that food shortages could be used by the power elite to coerce people in the future into accepting the controls (e.g., population control, political correctness, etc.) placed upon them in the new world order.

In his 1970 book, *Between Two Ages: America's Role in the Technetronic Era*, Zbigniew Brzezinski (CFR member and first director of the Trilateral Commission) had projected that in the technetronic society the trend seems to be toward ... effectively exploiting the latest communication techniques to manipulate emotions and control reason.... Human beings become increasingly manipulable and malleable, ... the increasing availability of biochemical means of human control, ... the possibility of extensive chemical mind control.... Within a few years the rebels in the more advanced countries who today have the most visibility will be joined by a new generation making its claim to power in government and business, ... accepting as routine managerial processes current innovations such as planning-programming-budgeting systems (PPBS).... A national information grid that will integrate existing electronic data banks is already being developed.... The projected world information grid, for which Japan, Western Europe, and the United States are most suited, could create the basis for a common educational program, for the adoption of common academic standards.... Today we are again witnessing the emergence of transnational elites. ... [whose] ties cut across national boundaries.... It is likely that before long the social elites of most of the more advanced countries will be highly internationalist or globalist in spirit and outlook.... The nation–state is gradually yielding its sovereignty.... Further progress will require greater American sacrifices. More intensive efforts to shape a new world monetary structure will have to be undertaken, with some consequent risk to the present relatively favorable American position.

Similarly, CFR member (and former Citicorp chairman) Walter Wriston in *The Twilight of Sovereignty* (1992) spoke of "a new world monetary standard" and "the new international monetary system" saying "there is no escaping the system" and explaining as follows:

The world can no longer be understood as a collection of national economies, [but] a single global economy.... A truly global economy will require concessions of national power and compromises of national sovereignty that seemed impossible a few years ago and which even now we can but partly imagine. ... The global [information] network will be internationalists in their outlook and will approve and encourage the worldwide erosion of traditional sovereignty.

In the European Union's April 1994 *Report on United States Barriers to Trade and Investment*, it states: "The comprehensive multilateral dispute settlement mechanism which has been agreed upon in the framework of the World Trade Organization will. . . . oblige [countries] to bring their domestic legislation into conformity with Uruguay Round agreements."

Article XVI, paragraph 4, of the WTO specifically states, "Each member shall ensure the conformity of its laws, regulations, and administrative procedures with its obligations," and that its dispute settlement board will be the final judge concerning whether the WTO's global rules of trade and tariffs have been met. All nations must abide by these judgments, and financial penalties and sanctions can be imposed if WTO's rules aren't met. The attorneys-general of forty-two states were so concerned about the WTO that they wrote a letter to President Clinton calling for a "State–Federal Consultation Summit" to consider the effect of the WTO upon state laws. The WTO would be the world socialists' dream come true, as the U.S. would have only one vote out of 123 nations (and no veto), and the majority of those nations are socialist in one form or another. More than three-fourths of them also voted against the U.S. on more than half of the U.N. votes in 1993. Malcolm S. Forbes, Jr., on "The Charlie Rose Show" (July 3, 1995) said regarding America's new trading relationship with Japan and other countries that it wasn't free trade, but rather the Clinton administration had adopted "managed trade, which is Socialism-like," and the Republicans went along with it.

Relevant to George Ridgeway's *Merchants of Peace* (1938, 1959) discussion of "economic disarmament" (where through technology transfers, countries are forced to become interdependent), the 1936 Communist International described their three-stage plan for world government: (1) Socialize the economies of all nations; (2) Bring about federal unions of various groupings of these socialized nations; and (3) Amalgamate the regional unions into a world union of socialist states. And later (March 1993) *World Trade* quoted crypto-Marxist Will Swaim opining that the new homogenized global economy "may become just the kind of grim, unthinkable place that Marx hoped it might: The launching pad for the worldwide socialist revolution."

I have for some time been indicating that the strategy of the global planners has been to form regional economic alliances (e.g., NAFTA, European Economic

Union, APEC, etc.), eventually merge them into a one-world economic system, and then argue that a world government is necessary to manage it. (Nov. 15, 1994, President Clinton in Asia agreed in the Asia-Pacific Economic Cooperation [APEC] forum to end trade restrictions in twenty-five years, and beginning in late 1994 the Clinton administration talked with the European Union about creating TAFTA, a Trans-Atlantic Free Trade Area. In early June 1995, Secretary of State Warren Christopher said regarding the idea of TAFTA: "We intend to give it the serious study it deserves, with its considerable potential to form an element of our overall strategy.... The long-term objective is the integration of the economies of North America and Europe, consistent with the principles of the World Trade Organization.") Evidence that this will happen now comes from a book, *Western Hemisphere Economic Integration* (1994), by Gary C. Hufbauer and Jeffrey Schott. The book is dedicated to David Rockefeller, and in it one reads:

> Once a group of countries liberalizes its trade in goods and services, the logic
> of economics and politics inevitably points to other elements of the integration
> agenda.... The greater the need for some institutional mechanism to administer
> the arrangements and to resolve the inevitable disputes, and the stronger the case
> for a common legal framework.

The "institutional mechanism" in all likelihood would be the World Trade Organization (WTO), and the "common legal framework" would eventually be a world government. And in case there is any doubt that the world government would be a redistribute-the-wealth socialist one, Hufbauer and Schott also write:

> In Europe, pronounced social disparities between members of the European
> Union are to some extent addressed through fiscal transfers from richer partners
> to poorer partners ... and they implicitly provide a quid pro quo for the ceding
> of sovereignty over trade and monetary policy to supraregional bodies.... Much
> depends on the political will to accept the "creative destruction" of local industries
> and jobs.... Each country has a different threshold of economic pain and different
> means of sharing that pain across social groups. Those thresholds and mechanisms
> will inevitably govern the inauguration and the pace of economic integration....

Autocratic regimes may be well-suited to force the inauguration of trade reforms, but a democratic regime seems better able to manage the political differences that inevitably arise from the resulting redistribution of income and dislocation of industries within the country.... Like the NAFTA before it, a Western Hemisphere Free Trade Association will not prompt the formation of antagonistic trade blocs in Europe, Asia, and the Western Hemisphere. Instead, it will prompt competitive liberalization and integration on a global basis....

This aim of economic "integration" can be seen from the following telling remark by David Rockefeller (at the U.N. Ambassadors' dinner) on September 14, 1994, when he emphasized that "... this present 'window of opportunity,' during which a truly peaceful and interdependent world order might be built, will not be open for long. Already there are powerful forces at work that threaten to destroy all of our hopes and efforts to erect an enduring structure of global cooperation."

Also relevant to both NAFTA and GATT are the remarks of *Economist* editorial director Nico Colchester regarding "the slow death of the nation–state" in that journal's special edition titled, "The World in 1995," in which he commented:

Great companies now transcend nationality. Elites do the same.... Although people may travel widely abroad and work for international companies and watch foreign television, they nonetheless need, at this stage of history, a sovereign state of their own to cling to as children do to a teddy bear.... Why should Washington bow to a Geneva-based Solomon when it can become the Brussels of its own continent? The smaller ambition is more attainable than the larger ideal. Both, however, are a dagger in the heart of dying national sovereignty.

And pertaining to the European Union (EU), *The (London) Times* (February 3, 1996) published Charles Bremner's article, "Nation State's Day Is Over, Britain Told," in which he stated: "Helmut Kohl, the German Chancellor, yesterday urged Europe to turn its back on the nation state.... [Kohl said] 'European integration is in reality a question of war and peace in the 21st century.' He endorsed the remark made last year by the late President Mitterand of France that 'nationalism is war.' ... [Kohl said] 'nationalism has brought great suffering to our continent.'"

When Felix Rohatyn, with international bankers Lazard Brothers, testified before the Senate Commerce Committee on November 15, 1994, he made it clear that powerful international interests had already planned on GATT's passage and had invested accordingly. Rohatyn then offered the veiled threat that if GATT didn't pass, there'd be dire economic consequences. And just before the Senate passed GATT on December 1, 1994, Senate commerce committee chairman Ernest Hollings said, "This GATT agreement is being pushed by David Rockefeller and the Trilateral Commission."

Members of the Trilateral Commission include international bankers and the heads of international companies and corporations. And perhaps relevant in that regard is the book, *Global Dreams: Imperial Corporations and the New World Order* (1994), by Richard Barnet and John Cavanagh (both with the leftist Institute for Policy Studies), who write in the book that "the balance of power in world politics has shifted in recent years from territorially bound governments to companies that can roam the world."

In a review of the book in the *Chicago Tribune* (March 27, 1994), *Tribune* senior writer R. C. Longworth noted that

> Global production is not beginning to employ the growing number of people who want jobs. Even those with jobs find that the pressures of globalization are pushing wages down. . . . This flow [of money], coupled with the ease with which companies move jobs around the globe, has shattered the ability of national governments to control their own economies. . . . The trends can only accelerate . . . [resulting in] even moral outrage . . . where traditional ways of life are under assault by international forces. This understandable reaction, by people who have lost control of their lives to vast impersonal forces, is no more than a futile gesture in a world where no country can afford the luxury of dropping out.

(This is worth remembering regarding GATT and WTO proponents' claim that the U.S. can simply withdraw from them if things don't go our way.)

Not only did David Rockefeller establish the Trilateral Commission but he has also been a prominent international banker for some time, and on ABC's "This Week with David Brinkley" August 28, 1994, commentator Cokie Roberts casually remarked that "global bankers are really running the world." This is not surprising given that we know Colonel House had close ties to J. P. Morgan and the old banking families of Europe (including Lazard Brothers?), and that the *Columbia Encyclopedia* (Third Edition, 1962, page 2334) indicates the Democratic nomination went to Woodrow Wilson in 1912 when William Jennings Bryan switched his support to Wilson, "prompted by Edward M. House." William McAdoo was Wilson's national campaign vice-chairman (whom Wilson as president would appoint as secretary of the treasury), and would later comment in *Crowded Years* (1931) regarding the 1912 campaign: "The fact is that there is a serious danger of this country becoming a pluto-democracy; that is, a sham republic with the real government in the hands of small clique of enormously wealthy men, who speak through their money, and whose influence, even today, radiates to every corner of the United States."

We know that "the powers that be" have not only supported other Democratic nominees (like FDR) besides Wilson, but Republicans as well. To the global planners, neither liberalism nor conservatism, Democrats nor Republicans, are important, but rather power and control. Relevant to socialism is George Orwell's *1984* describing a "newspeak" language including "doublethink," exemplified in the slogans of "the party," such as "Freedom is slavery. Ignorance is strength." Orwell explained that "newspeak has been devised to meet the ideological needs of Ingsoc, or English socialism," and "Big Brother" represents neither the failed German Nazis (National Socialists) nor the Russian communists (Union of Soviet Socialist Republics) who would fail (*1984* was written in 1949), but rather "the Party" which will control men's minds. "Big Brother's" representative in the book reveals: "The rule of the Party is forever. . . . The Party seeks power entirely for its own sake. . . . We are interested solely in power. . . . We are priests of power."

Orwell, whose real name was Eric Blair, probably got the title of *1984* either from the centenary of the founding of the Fabian Society in 1884 or from Jack London's prediction in *The Iron Heel* (1907) of when fascism might come to the U.S. By 1978, over 100 of Orwell's 137 predictions in *1984* had come true, such as books written by computer, forced metrification, three dimensional effects in art, machines that translate voice into print, and the merging of gender identities (*The Futurist,* December 1978).

At this point, you are probably wondering how, just a few years after President

George H. W. Bush declared a "new world order" and General Norman Schwartz-kopf prosecuted the war against Saddam Hussein, can we be thinking that the power elite are moving toward global control just because someone named Rohatyn from something called Lazard Brothers makes a veiled threat about dire global economic consequences if GATT wasn't passed. This is where a brief history lesson is in order. Felix Rohatyn was one of those considered by President Clinton as his first secretary of the treasury (his treasury secretary designate as of December 22, 1994, was Robert Rubin, a trustee of the Carnegie Corporation of New York who did postgraduate work at the Fabian Socialists' London School of Economics, 1960–61).

Cecil Rhodes' plan for world domination was initiated through Round Table Groups (semi-secret discussion and lobbying groups), with a small group in the U.S. composed of Walter Lippman, Thomas Lamont (of J. P Morgan & Co.), and others. The first international leaders of the group were Lord Alfred Milner and Lionel Curtis, and operating funds came from those associated with J. P. Morgan, the Rockefellers, the Lazard Brothers and others. Oil was a key source of revenue, as the world oil cartel was formed by a September 17, 1928, agreement among Standard Oil (Rockefeller), Royal Dutch–Shell (House of Orange originally, and historically important in events leading toward a new world order), and Anglo–Iranian (AIOC). But Iran nationalized its oil production, and CIA director Allen Dulles directed the overthrow of the Iranian government in August 1953 through $10 million in secret CIA funds he gave to Col. H. Norman Schwartzkopf (General Schwartzkopf's father) for that purpose. Dulles had been a director of the Schroeder Bank in New York and an old associate of Frank Tiarks, a director of Lazard Brothers Bank and a partner in the Schroeder Bank of London (according to Prof. Carroll Quigley, "the Schroeder Bank in Cologne helped arrange Hitler's accession to power as chancellor in January 1933"). It was at about this time that Robert H. (Lord) Brand (brother-in-law of Lady Astor) succeeded Lionel Curtis as international head of the Round Table Groups until his death in 1963. He was managing director of Lazard Brothers, and he was succeeded in 1963 by Adam Marris as both head of the Round Table Groups and managing director of Lazard Brothers Bank. Thus the importance of Felix Rohatyn's statement representing Lazard Brothers before the U.S. Senate Commerce Committee in late 1994. Coincidentally, the Trilateralist Rohatyn has been on the board of Pfizer, Inc. along with Lazard Brothers senior advisor James

T. Lynn (Trilateralist), Chase Manhattan Bank (with Trilateralist Commission founder David Rockefeller as international advisory chairman) CEO and chairman Thomas Labrecque (Trilateralist and a New York Federal Reserve director), Pfizer CEO and chairman William Steere, Jr. (a New York Federal Reserve director), and Ryder Systems (Ryder trucks, like those coincidentally used in the Oklahoma City bombing, and in the World Trade Center bombing according to the *New York Times,* March 5, 1993) CEO and chairman M. Anthony Burns (Trilateralist on the board of Chase Manhattan Bank).

Remember though that the one-worlders not only want political and economic control, but religious control as well. In this regard, an indirect attack upon religious freedom would have more likelihood of success, and on November 16, 1993, Congress overwhelmingly passed Public Law 103–141, the "Religious Freedom Restoration Act." Seeming to protect religious freedom, part of the act stated that "governments should not substantially burden religious exercise without compelling justification."

However, upon closer examination, what this language actually does is obliterate the language in the First Amendment to our Constitution, which provides that "Congress shall make no law respecting an establishment of religion, or prohibiting the free exercise thereof."

To be sure, federal courts have already been undermining that language for years, but those decisions could have always been reversed in the future. Now, though, there is actually a public law that indicates governments can "substantially burden religious exercise" if there is a "compelling justification," however they choose to interpret that.

But for the world socialist government to exercise complete control, monitoring of nations' and individuals' activities will have to occur. That is why the "Treaty on Open Skies" is important. An Associated Press story on August 30, 1994, related how the treaty would allow about twenty-seven countries to take low-altitude and high-altitude photographs of U.S. (and any other nations') military installations. The treaty would also provide that no area of any country would be off-limits, and therefore anything and anyone could be monitored.

Concerning the monitoring of individuals, *USA Today* (June 6, 1995) published "Embedded Electronics, A Chip Off Sci-Fi," in which one reads that "in the near future, people may have chips implanted under their skin with medical history information, even X-ray and MRI-images, says chip designer Fadi Kurdahl, University of California, Irvine. . . . Scientists and researchers also are working on fusing computer technology into the brain, . . . 'chip grafting' [that] involves an implanted chip that could translate and digitize thoughts." In *Popular Science* (July 1995), Ronald Kane was quoted by Phil Patton as saying, "If we had our way, we'd implant a chip behind everyone's ear in the maternity ward." Kane is vice-president of Cubic Corporation's automatic revenue collection group (Cubic, according to Patton, "is the leading maker of smart card systems for mass transit systems, highway tolls, parking and other applications.").

On ABC's "20/20" (September 1, 1995) Hugh Downs said: "Big Brother has finally arrived [overseas]. . . . People are being watched from cameras half-a-mile away." Reporter Lynn Sherr then related that,

> surveillance cameras are being used to patrol entire [more than 100] British com-
> munities. . . . These are the omnipresent eyes of the law. . . . It's the Big Brother
> issue. . . . A police chief in Scotland says: "When crime and when disorder and
> when people's fears become so acute that they are crying out for something to be
> done about it, then perhaps they have to give up just a little bit more of [their]
> freedoms in order to counteract it."

Barbara Walters told Lynn Sherr, "I think I'm for it [widespread video surveil-lance]."

And in Raleigh, North Carolina, there have been video monitors in strategic locations at the Halifax Court Apartments complex because it has been a high crime area. The video images have been relayed to a police substation, and the residents loved it because it was seen as reducing criminal activity there. While that was probably true, one can't help but be reminded of how the reader is told in George Orwell's *1984* that "you will come to love 'Big Brother,'" who video-monitors the people. Orwell modeled some of his book after Yevgeny Zamyatin's *We* (written in 1920), in which "The One State" under "The Benefactor" (with his "socratically-bald head") gained complete control over the world in the twenty-first century. Freedom was eliminated in "The One State." "Reason" prevailed. Everyone was known by a consonant and odd number (males) or a vowel and even number (females) instead of by names. And all work was "group activity" (as in some outcome-based education today) to ensure unanimity of thought.

Zamyatin's *We* focuses on Russia, which is relevant concerning Orwell's statement that "you will come to love 'Big Brother,' " in that recently old hard-liners (now calling themselves "democratic socialists") actually have been put back into power by the people in Lithuania, Poland, etc. On PBS' "Washington Week in Review" (December 30, 1994), Georgie Anne Geyer said Boris Yeltsin "can't last" and will be replaced by a more "nationalistic" person.

Could it be that Mikhail Gorbachev, like the fictional phoenix rising from the ashes, will be voted back into power by the Russian people, who can't stand their current economic chaos (organized crime, black markets, etc.) and have "come to love Big Brother's" order? Gorbachev still proudly calls himself a socialist and heads the International Green Cross, which collaborated with the Earth Council and Rio "Earth Summit" secretary-general Maurice Strong to write the Earth Charter, which would create an international environmental regulatory code.

In March 2000, the Earth Charter Commission meeting at UNESCO headquarters approved the final version of the Earth Charter, which was later presented to the U.N. in the Ark of Hope (designed like the biblical Ark of the Covenant, see www.ark-of-hope.org/home.html). And on June 25, 2001, the U.S. Conference of Mayors passed a resolution stating that the conference "endorses the Earth Charter and commits the organization to the realization of its aim." Among the Earth Charter's goals is to "promote the equitable distribution of wealth within nations and among nations"—in other words, socialism!

Although President Ronald Reagan in the 1980s had removed the U.S. from UNESCO, on October 3, 2003, under President George W. Bush, U.S. Secretary of Education Rod Paige in Paris stated: "The United States is pleased to return to UNESCO.... Our governments have entrusted us with the responsibility of preparing our children to become citizens of the world." The problem with the concept of "world citizens" is that the term "citizen" implies a legal obligation. If one is a "citizen" of a state, one must obey state law. Therefore, if one is a "world citizen," one must obey "world law."

Returning to Gorbachev, remember that several years ago, he (and Eduard

Shevardnadze) talked of "one European home ... from the Atlantic to Vladivostok." And on November 19, 1991, Shevardnadze stated that "the building of a United Europe, a great United Europe from the Atlantic to Vladivostok, including all our territory, is inevitable. We will build a united military space as well—we will build a united Europe based on the principles of collective security."

This "collective security" is supposed to occur under the Conference on Security and Cooperation in Europe (CSCE) with fifty-six members, headquartered in Prague, and dominated by Russia with their hope that it will subsume NATO. On September 24, 1995 the *Washington Post* printed an article, "Global Chic: Gorby's Bash by the Bay," in which author George Cothran proposed that "maybe challenging the powers-that-be isn't Gorbachev's main objective. Rather than disrupting the hide-bound elites that run the world, the former Soviet president seems more intent on rejoining their exclusive club." Beginning three days later, on September 27 (through October 1), 1995, Mikhail Gorbachev was convening chairman and host of the "State of the World Forum: Toward a New Civilization," which "analyzed the current state of the world and articulated the fundamental principles of politics and values necessary to constructively shape the early 21st century," according to the Gorbachev Foundation.

That Geyer said "nationalistic" is important, because before there can be the "international socialism" of the new world order world government, there has to be "national socialism" (which is what the word Nazi stood for) in the nations of the world. In that regard, American government official Sumner Welles in 1944 wrote *The Time for Decision,* in chapter nine of which he revealed that the German general staff "made detailed plans for a later renewal of its attempt to dominate the world.... when the favorable moment arrives.... [perhaps] two generations from now" (1990s). Welles goes on to say "half the mechanism is secret and will so remain," and involves the theory of

> indirect complicity. . . . in three principal ways: (a) It will try to create doubts among the people of each country as to the ability, integrity, wisdom, or loyalty of their leading statesmen; (b) in critical moments it will attempt to paralyze or to diminish the capacity for cool thinking by the people as a whole; and (c) it will search in each country for men who, through ambition, vanity, or personal interest,

will be disposed to serve the causes.... Agents of the German General Staff have already been naturalized, usually in two successive countries, so that their future activities will be less suspect. The majority of them are being trained to appear as men of large commercial or financial interests.... over a period of years [gaining] a controlling influence in labor unions, in the banking world, in Chambers of Commerce, and, through these channels, an indirect influence in the press.... When the right time comes, stimulate internal dissension sufficiently to destroy the morale of the people in those countries marked as victims.

Relevant to the activities of the Nazis after World War II, from 1968 to 1972 former Nazi Paul Dickopf would be president of Interpol. And from 1972 to 1982, former Nazi Kurt Waldheim would be U.N. secretary–general. Welles explained that centralizing government authority at the national level is the key to stereotyping the education of youth, weakening the ability of individual citizens to think for themselves, and making possible official encroachment upon liberties (including religious freedom), according to the plan.

But how would the process work? How could citizens' (especially youths') values be changed? In *Psychology Today* (September 1971), Milton Rokeach wrote "Persuasion That Persists," in which he revealed:

Suppose you could take a group of people, give them a twenty-minute pencil-and-paper task, talk to them for ten to twenty minutes afterward, and thereby produce long-range changes in core values and personal behavior in a significant portion of this group. For openers, it would of course have major implications for education, government, propaganda, and therapy.... My colleagues and I have in the last five years achieved the kinds of results suggested in the first paragraph of this article. ... It now seems to be within man's power to alter experimentally another person's basic values, and to control the direction of the change.

Rokeach went on to explain the use of "dissonance" (what John Dewey called a "felt difficulty"), and how he and his colleagues didn't use the process of exposing a person to conflicting attitudes or values held by other persons who are in some way important to the first person, but rather they used another technique, exposing a person "to information designed to make him consciously aware of inconstancies within his own value-attitude system" (in schools, values clarification techniques such as leading students to particular value changes by using a series of socratic leading questions).

Relevant to "indirect" attacks upon our values is signer of the 1973 *Humanist Manifesto* Sidney Hook's statement in *The Humanist* (January–February 1977): "Human beings can be influenced to examine critically their religious beliefs only by indirection, (by which) I mean the development of a critical attitude in all our educational institutions that will aim to make students less credulous to claims that trancend their reflective experience."

Could it be that through future crises (e.g., economic, crime, etc.) in the U.S., the people (having "critically examined their own religious beliefs") will actually be willing to sacrifice certain of their God-given freedoms in order for big (socialist) goverment ("Big Brother") to maintain "order" (e.g., safety, economic stability, etc.)?

What might happen? Congressman Charles A. Lindbergh (father of the famous aviator) said that the Panic of 1907 was used by "the Money Trust" to "squeeze out of business" those not favorable to them, and to frighten people "into demanding changes in the banking and currency laws which the Money Trust would frame." Thus, just as the Panic of 1907 (stock market crash, followed by bank failures, followed by massive unemployment and inflation) led to the people accepting a Federal Reserve, a similar pattern (stock market crash of 1929, etc.) led to the Great Depression of the 1930s and the people's willingness to accept FDR's socialistic programs. Thus, the power elite may believe that an international financial crisis today could lead the people to accept global economic controls (with a world currency) and a socialist world government which would "care for" (and control) them from cradle to grave.

The people may actually, voluntarily, ask Big Brother to take charge of their lives (socialism), as in Orwell's *1984,* Big Brother's agent, O'Brien, said: "We are not content with negative obedience, nor even with the most abject submission. When finally you surrender to us, it must be of your own free will. We do not destroy the heretic because he resists us. . . . We convert him, we capture his inner mind, we reshape him."

This is similar to the Fabian socialists' motto: "Remould it [the world] nearer to the heart's desire."

What is in store for the world was proclaimed about fifty years ago by the Jesuit, Pierre Teilhard de Chardin, listed in *The Aquarian Conspiracy* by Marilyn Ferguson as the person leading New Agers indicated most often as having "a profound influence upon their thinking." He advocated a one-world government and "that the proposed organization must be international and in the end totalitarian." He also related that a group of elect people would engage in eugenics, and further stated: "We have only to believe, then little by little, we shall see the universal horror unbend, and then smile upon us, and then take us in its more than human arms."

The "horror" for the children burned or suffocated alive in Waco, Texas, occurred in 1993. And following the tragedy, on April 20 President Clinton insensitively said attorney-general Janet Reno (who ordered the raid) should not resign just "because some religious fanatics murdered themselves." No one has ever explained why the raid was ordered for the one day, out of months before and after the event, that there was a forty mile-per-hour wind that spread the consuming fire so rapidly, and few escaped.

On "This Morning" (CBS) August 25, 1994, was described a new supercomputer soon coming to the U.S. It is named "GOD," and contains all vital medical statistics, so that it can determine whether patients should be kept alive or not, based upon health and economic factors. This calls to mind the statement by leading Fabian socialist George Bernard Shaw in *The Intelligent Woman's Guide to Socialism and Capitalism* (1928), in which he revealed that ".... under Socialism you would not be allowed to be poor. You would be forcibly fed, clothed, lodged, taught, and employed whether you liked it or not. If it were discovered that you had not the character and industry enough to be worth all this trouble, you might possibly be executed in a kindly manner...."

We've already had a glimpse of the eugenic future, as Allan Chase (author of *The Legacy of Malthus* in 1976) reported that up to 1974, the U.S. compulsorily sterilized more people than Nazi Germany. Commenting on this in "Social Cleansing" (*New Statesman & Society*, August 5, 1994), Alexander Cockburn wrote that

The keenest of these cleansers were Northern liberals.... Eugenic sterilization was most energetically pushed by progressive politicians, medical experts and genteel women's groups. . . . At this fraught moment [1994], the White House is tipping its hat to the social cleansers. . . . Wait for the social cleansers—aka Nazis—to start insisting that poor black teenagers accept Norplant as a condition for any form of social benefit, or for living in public housing, or for existing.

Cockburn refers to Justice Oliver Wendell Holmes' 1927 Supreme Court decision upholding forced sterilization; and after Holmes "complacently" told fellow eugenicist (and Fabian socialist) Harold Laski about it, Laski wrote back to Holmes (May 7, 1927): "Sterilize *all* the unfit, among whom I include *all* fundamentalists."

Thus it will be, under the new world order's world socialist government when it has gained complete control, which may not be in the too distant future. Concerning the growing power of the U.S. government over its people, a Gallup poll taken in April 1995 found that nearly 40 percent of those surveyed felt "the federal government has become so large and powerful, it poses an immediate threat to the rights and freedoms of ordinary citizens." (A *Time*/CNN poll the first week in May 1995 found that 52 percent of Americans believe that government poses "a threat to the rights and freedom of citizens.") Globally, the new world order's world socialist government will be operationally characterized as what I have called "technological feudalism" or "techno-feudalism." Relevant to this term are comments from Alvin Toffler's *Powershift: Knowledge, Wealth, and Violence at the Edge of the 21st Century* (1990), in which he projected:

. . . we may well be circling back to the kind of world system that existed before industrialism, before political power was packaged into clearly defined national entities. That pre-smokestack world was a hodgepodge of . . . feudal princedoms, religious movements, and other entities, all scrambling for power and asserting rights. . . . We are now moving back to a more heterogeneous system again—only in a fast-changing world of high technology. . . . This is an immense leap that . . . propels religion once more to the center of the global stage. . . .

(See pages 121–123 at the back of my book here quoting W. J. Ghent.)

This time, however, the global planners intend for socialism to be the "religion" of the new world order, just as Antonio Gramsci remarked in May 1916: "Socialism is precisely the religion that must overwhelm Christianity." In *The New Order* (1919–1925), the Marxist humanist Gramsci explained that socialism would triumph by first capturing the culture via infiltration of schools, universities, churches, the media, and other societal and religious institutions. Rather than a direct assault, he advocated a process resulting in an evolutionary transition to socialism by transforming the consciousness of society, eventually resulting in a socialist elite ruling the world.

Recall that Fabian socialist H. G. Wells wrote in *The Shape of Things to Come* (1933) that although the world government "had been plainly coming for some years, although it has been endlessly feared and murmured against, it found no opposition prepared anywhere."

That will be because mankind will have been conditioned to love the "universal horror" of Big Brother controlling everyone's lives, "caring" for all their needs from cradle to grave, within a world socialist government. And evidence that this time is fast approaching has come from the U.N. International Conference on Population and Development (Cairo, September 1994), where U.S. Agency for International Development director (and CFR member) J. Brian Atwood proclaimed regarding the ICPD's assumptions and designs, including population control: "In time, individuals will change their outlook. Societies will change their mores. Religions will interpret their beliefs differently. . . . And governments will change their policies."

Remember that Aldous Huxley in *The Devils of Loudun* (1952) stated: "Assemble a mob of men and women previously conditioned by a daily reading of newspapers; treat them to amplified band music, bright lights . . . and in next to no time you can reduce them to a state of almost mindless subhumanity. Never before have so few been in a position to make fools, maniacs or criminals of so many."

Concerning Huxley's reference to "bright lights," one reads in *The Body Electric* (1985) by Robert Becker, M.D. and Gary Selden: "Hypnotists often use a strobe light, flashing at alpha-wave frequencies to ease the glide into trance." Extra-low frequency waves can tranquilize and enhance suggestibility, and have you noticed recent TV ads use flashing lights and quickly changing images? These "highlighted moments" of unusual images (e.g., swirling tennis shoes or people), according to

Bill Strittmatter, put the mind in an "information absorption mode" (as when one hears a gunshot) rather than a "thinking" or analytic mode.

Prior to the Cairo conference, according to nationally syndicated columnist Robert Novak (*Colorado Springs Gazette-Telegraph,* September 7, 1994), U.S. undersecretary of state Tim Wirth (who has been a CFR member) said regarding underdeveloped countries where abortion is prohibited by law: "A government which is violating basic human rights" (e.g., abortion rights) "should not hide behind the defense of sovereignty."

Concerning U.S. taxes, Indianapolis mayor Stephen Goldsmith addressing the National Taxpayers Conference on November 18, 1994, said: "Our tax code says we prefer socialism over capitalism."

And to pay for the coming world socialist government, it is noteworthy that a global income tax was on the agenda for the U.N. World Summit for Social Development in Copenhagen, Denmark, March 6–12, 1995, A.D. and a report proposing a series of international taxes to support the U.N. was also prepared for (and financed by the Ford Foundation) Secretary–General Boutros Boutros-Ghali. He was formerly a member of the central committee of the Political Bureau of the Arab Socialist Union, who was on May 22, 1990, elected as vice president of Socialist International (as has been Gro Harlem Brundtland, former prime minister of Norway, who was elected director-general of the World Health Organization on January 27, 1998) until his resignation in late 1991 when he was elected U.N. secretary-general. (Zbigniew Brzezinski, in his 1970 book *Between Two Ages,* referred "to the possibility of something along the lines of a global taxation system.")

Remember when you read Revelation 13:16-17, "And he causeth all . . . to receive a mark in their right hand . . . and that no man might buy or sell, save he that had the mark [of the beast]," that the *London Daily Mail* (June 24, 1993) had a full-page article with a graphic of a woman in the European Union buying grocery or department store items by placing a finger or palm of her hand on a computer scanner to identify her at the check-out counter. A little later, in Revelation 16:16, is mentioned the battle of Armageddon, and noteworthy in that regard is that after the recent end of the "Cold War," the Pentagon developed seven possible scenarios regarding the future, the last one of which was that "out of the former Soviet Union or some combination of powerful nations, a new, anti-democratic and expansionist superpower emerges to threaten U.S. interests, calling for a total mobilization for global war in the year 2001" (See *New York Times,* February 17, 1992, p. A8).

Many were encouraged by the results of the 1994 elections, but it must be remembered that many Republicans (even supposedly conservative Rep. Phil Crane) supported NAFTA, GATT, and even Most Favored Nation status for the brutal dictators in China (would they have done the same for Hitler?). In addition to President Clinton favoring MFN status for China, and the passage of GATT with its World Trade Organization, GATT and the WTO were also supported by Speaker of the House Newt Gingrich (member of the CFR and the World Future Society, who was on the executive committee of the Congressional Clearinghouse on the Future for a number of years) and Senate majority leader Robert Dole. Dole has been closely tied to Archer-Daniels-Midland head Dwayne Andreas, who first visited the Soviet Union in 1952 and would later say "Gorbachev and I go hand in hand." Andreas would also be described by the *Wall Street Journal* as gaining "an apparent position as Kremlin favorite" American businessman. According to *The New Yorker,* February 16, 1987, when Andreas visited Africa in the 1960s, he said: "Wherever we went, the national leaders seemed to have been educated in Europe and influenced by the socialist leanings of the London School of Economics. . . . They were trying to nationalize industries that hadn't yet come into being. I urged them, while I was there, to wait fifty years and then take them over.".

On ABC's "This Week with David Brinkley" (November 13, 1994), Sen. Daniel Patrick Moynihan said the upcoming vote on GATT would be "the most important vote of this decade."

In the Ways and Means Committee transcripts of the hearings on GATT and the WTO in the U.S. House, Newt Gingrich stated that he was leaning toward voting for the treaty, but

> I am just saying that we need to be honest about the fact that we are transferring from the United States at a practical level significant authority to a new organization. This is a transformational moment. I would feel better if the people who favor this would just be honest about the scale of change. . . . This is not just another trade agreement. This is adopting something which twice, once in the 1940s and once in the 1950s, the U.S. Congress rejected. . . . I think we have to be very care-

ful, because it is a very big transfer of power. Now, yes, we could in theory take the power back.... But the fact is we are not likely to disrupt the entire world trading system [by pulling out]. And, therefore, we ought to be very careful, because we are not likely to take it back.

Gingrich (who has said he has "an enormous personal ambition") is a very close friend of futurists Alvin and Heidi Toffler, who wrote about social changes that effect values, family structure, religion, etc., in *Creating a New Civilization: The Politics of the Third Wave,* commended by Newt Gingrich who (on C-Span) said:"In this 100 pages you'll begin to sense what the twenty-first century America, the twenty-first century government, and the twenty-first century Congress need to be."

What this 1994 Gingrich-endorsed book says "needs to be" is the Third Wave new civilization "based on new, non-nuclear families." The Tofflers in the book (published by The Progress & Freedom Foundation, with a foreword by Gingrich) say it is futile to speak of Second Wave

> values, as though one could return to the values and morality of the 1950s.... We will need to prepare people for work in such fields as human services [child care, domestic work, etc.].... Majority rule is increasingly obsolete. It is not majorities, but minorities that count. ... The Constitution of the U.S. needs to be altered. ... The system must die and be replaced.... Nationalism is [Second Wave] ... as economies are transformed by the Third Wave, they are compelled to surrender part of their sovereignty.

On March 1, 1995, speaking at the Nixon Center for Peace and Freedom, Gingrich stated that the Third Wave "will dissolve much of what we have thought of as the nation-state."

In the dialectic, it is important for the global elite to control both ends of the political spectrum. In Professor Quigley's *Tragedy and Hope,* he wrote historically regarding business interests that

> they expected that they would be able to control both political parties equally. Indeed, some of them intended to contribute to both and allow an alternation of the two parties in public office in order to conceal their own influence, inhibit any

exhibition of independence by politicians, and allow the electorate to believe that they were exercising their own free choice.

Curtis Dall in *F.D.R.: My Exploited Father-in-Law* likewise related:

> It appears to me that politics is the gentle art of having to pretend to be something that you know you are not, for vote-catching purposes, while being aided by our press. . . . Usually, carefully screened leading "actors" are picked well in advance of election day by a small group, picked for *both major parties*. . . . It is desirable for [candidates] to have great *personal ambition* and, perchance, to be *vulnerable to blackmail*. . . . [Colonel House knew Woodrow Wilson was vulnerable to blackmail] . . . for some past occurrences; hence, someone not apt to become too independent in time. . . .

Relevant here are Alvin Gouldner's comments in his "Taking Over" chapter in Warren Bennis' book *American Bureaucracy* (1970), in which Gouldner states:

> Those finally chosen as the successor are sponsored by men powerful in the organization, by men who may have followed and supported their careers in the systems ever since they came into it. . . . If [one] is going down, be assured, someone is greasing the skids; if he is going up, there are—with equal certainty—some who are helping to pull and to push him up.

Bennis concludes the book by pronouncing that "change is the 'godhead' term for our age as it has not been for any other. The phrase 'the only constant is change' has reached the point of a cliche, which at once anesthetizes us to its pain and stimulates grotesque fantasies about a Brave New World with no place in the sun for us."

That the global planning elite are directing this "change" is evident from FDR's son (Elliott Roosevelt), who wrote in *The Conservators* (1983) that "there are within our world perhaps only a dozen organizations which shape the courses of our various destinies as rigidly as they regularly constituted governments . . . this unofficial council of the elite, the creme de la creme of global planners."

Similarly, in *Democratic Dictatorship: The Emergent Constitution of Control* (1981), Arthur S. Miller described a "new feudal order" (see relevant chart on page 127 of my book here) controlled by elitists, and asserted that "dictatorship will come—is coming—but with the acquiescence of the people. . . . The goal is 'predictable' man."

Miller further explained in *The Secret Constitution and the Need for Constitutional Change* (1987), sponsored in part by the Rockefeller Foundation, that

> a pervasive system of thought control exists in the United States. . . . The citizenry is indoctrinated by employment of the mass media and the system of public education. . . . People are told what to think *about*. . . . The old order is crumbling. . . . Nationalism should be seen as a dangerous social disease. . . . A new vision is required to plan and manage the future, a global vision that will transcend national boundaries and eliminate the poison of nationalistic "solutions." . . . A new Constitution is necessary. . . . Americans really have no choice, for constitutional alteration will come whether or not it is liked or planned for. . . . Ours is the age of the planned society. . . . No other way is possible.

And what would be the result of all this in terms of government? On June 14, 1992, on ABC's "This Week with David Brinkley," former top Reagan adviser Michael Deaver announced that "in five years [1997], we're going to have a World Parliament." (The above four quotations came from *The Network of Power and Part II (of) The New World Order: Chronology and Commentary* by Dennis Laurence Cuddy and Robert Henry Goldsborough.) Interestingly, in the January 1995 edition of *Harper's,* the World Constitution and Parliament Association placed a full-page ad presenting a "Manifesto" which "shall go into full force and effect upon confirmation at the Fourth Session of the Provisional World Parliament to convene in June, 1996." This "Manifesto," announced in January 1995, proclaimed that "the oceans and seabeds of earth are made the common property of all residents of Earth, together with the airspace above, Antarctica and Earth's moon. All are included within World Federation. Ownership is lodged on behalf of humanity in the Federal World Government organized under the Constitution for the Federation of Earth, with the World Parliament to which both the people of Earth and the National Governments elect delegates. . . . "

For the first thirty years or so of the twentieth century, the "facilitator" of the world planners was Colonel Edward M. House, who was "dialectically" close to the leading international bankers but also authored a book promoting "socialism as dreamed of by Karl Marx." For the middle of the century, the "facilitator" was John J. McCloy (CFR chairman 1953–1970, chairman of the Ford Foundation, and president of the World Bank, the latter of which would have James Wolfensohn as its president and chairman beginning in 1995 after President Clinton nominated him. According to a March 13, 1995, *New York Times* article by Peter Truell, Wolfensohn had been in an "investment banking partnership with Lord Rothschild of Britain." And President Clinton's 49th birthday party on August 19, 1995, was held at Wolfensohn's home, after Clinton vacationed at the estate of Sen. John D. Rockefeller IV.

John J. McCloy "dialectically" sat in Hitler's box at the 1936 Olympics and some years later was smiling and swimming with Khrushchev. In the 1950s, McCloy (and later others, like David Rockefeller) began to groom Henry Kissinger to "facilitate" the coming new world order. He "dialectically" prosecuted the war in Vietnam while also opening the door to communist China for President Nixon. And about twenty years later, in the July 18, 1993, *Los Angeles Times,* Kissinger strongly urged the passage of NAFTA saying: "What Congress will have before it is not a conventional trade agreement but the architecture of a new international system. . . . It would be a disaster if U.S. actions encouraged the re-emergence of nationalistic candidates. . . . The trade agreement is . . . a first step toward the new world order."

The passage of NAFTA was a key reason why the global planners wanted Bill Clinton to be president, because unlike George H. W. Bush, Clinton could appeal to Democrats' party loyalty and gain 40 percent of their vote which was necessary for passage. Without NAFTA, there could be no merging of regional economic alliances into a world economy which would have to be managed by a world government. That NAFTA would not result in all that its proponents claimed would be evidenced by NBC's chief economics correspondent Irving R. Levine's report (December 29, 1994) that

> the peso's fall makes U.S. goods more expensive in Mexico, cutting into sales and threatening the jobs of U.S. workers who make those goods. By contrast, the weakened peso makes Mexican goods cheaper in the U.S. and easier to sell. . . . None of

this was supposed to happen under the North American Free Trade Agreement, which was intended to create more U.S. exports and jobs.

But this didn't matter to the planning elite, as Clinton on January 31, 1995, marching to the tune of the international bankers issued an executive order loaning $20 billion to Mexico despite public opposition and congressional reservations. (Was the peso devaluation debacle an "accident," when one realizes multinational corporations that moved factories from the U.S. to Mexico just profited from the peso devaluation by having Mexican workers' pay cut 30–50 percent? The U.S. Commerce Department indicated 20,000 U.S. manufacturing jobs were lost to Mexico in February 1995 alone! And on May 3, 1995, Congressman Peter DeFazio said the lowering of wages and living standards on both sides of the border may have been the multinational corporations' and Wall Street's plan all along.) And domestically, Clinton was useful to the planning elite in naming two of only three U.S. Circuit Court of Appeals judges (Ruth Ginsberg and Stephen Breyer), who were CFR members, to the U.S. Supreme Court (thereby assuring protection of *Roe v. Wade* abortion rights).

Thus the connection between the Clinton presidency and the world government planners seems clear, but what about socialism? The brother-in-law of Strobe Talbott (mentioned in this book's introduction) is Derek Shearer, who has been a close friend and advisor of Bill Clinton. And in 1980, Shearer co-authored a book, *Economic Democracy,* emphasizing a "vision" and "change" and promoting what many understand to be a move toward socialism in America (e.g., national health care and insurance). The book outlined a plan for a Democrat who would implement these policies to run for the presidency. However, Clinton was only temporarily useful to "the powers that be."

Could it be that Clinton's liabilities would actually be useful in creating a great congressional turnover in the 1994 elections? The vote on GATT did not occur prior to the election, nor after the new Congress convened in 1995, when members would have been more accountable to the electorate. Rather it occurred in the lame duck session at the end of 1994 when defeated members of Congress, not beholden to voters who ousted them, could have been induced by various rewards to vote for GATT. Perhaps relevant here is Prof. Carroll Quigley's statement in *Tragedy and Hope* that the powers of financial capitalism had [a] far-reaching aim, nothing less than to create a world system of financial control in private hands able to dominate the political system of each country and the economy of the world as a whole. This system was to be controlled in a feudalist fashion by the central banks of the world acting in concert, by secret agreements arrived at in frequent meetings and conferences. The apex of the systems was to be the Bank for International Settlements [built in the shape of a boot, and in Orwell's *1984,* a description of the future under "Big Brother" is given as "a boot stamping on a human face—forever"].

Quigley continued, saying that the BIS was

in Basel, Switzerland, a private bank owned and controlled by the world's central banks which were themselves private corporations. Each central bank . . . sought to dominate its government by its ability to control Treasury loans, to manipulate foreign exchanges, to influence the level of economic activity in the country, and to influence cooperative politicians by subsequent economic rewards in the business world.

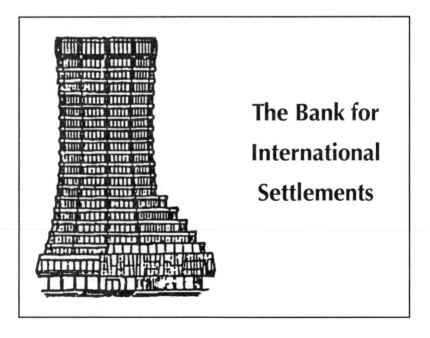

The Bank for International Settlements

New York Times reporter Keith Bradsher in that newspaper on August 5, 1995, wrote: "In a small Swiss city sits an international organization so obscure and secretive. . . . Control of the institution, the Bank for International Settlements, lies with some of the world's most powerful and least visible men: the heads of 32 central banks, officials able to shift billions of dollars and alter the course of economies at the stroke of a pen."

Remember that FDR is said to have once remarked that nothing happens politically by accident, but if it happened, it was planned that way.

In the mid–1990s, Henry Kissinger began to express his "displeasure" with Clinton in the press and media. It was time for "change," and it fit what Prof. Quigley said above about the possible control of both political parties and "an alternation of the two parties in public office." Another "change" was described by CFR member of Kissinger Associates, Lawrence Eagleburger. According to the *Daily Universe* (Brigham Young University campus newspaper), Eagleburger speaking at a BYU forum November 8, 1994, said the U.S. "can either become the world policeman, or an international policing force must be established with adequate authority and force to maintain world peace. . . . We have to be the world's thought policemen to create a world police force."

That the CFR has been important in this regard for some time is evident from Joseph Kraft's article, "School for Statesmen," published in *Harper's Magazine,* July 1958, in which he wrote that

> the Council plays a special part in helping to bridge the gap between the two parties, affording unofficially a measure of continuity when the guard changes in Washington. . . . In theory at least, the Council comes close to being an organ of what C. Wright Mills has called the Power Elite—a group of men, similar in interest and outlook, shaping events from invulnerable positions behind the scenes. . . . It has been called "the government in exile."

And to show the extent of their power "behind the scenes," a teletype from the FBI office in New York to J. Edgar Hoover dated February 10, 1972, and stamped "Confidential" and "Urgent," said concerning the CFR: ". . . Officers of the organization have included such prominent individuals as Allen W. Dulles, David Rockefeller and W. Averill Harriman.... As can be seen from characterization of Council and its activities it is probable classified US Government documents are maintained at Council for study and research."

That this "non-governmental" organization had "probable classified US Government documents" tells a great deal. And that their power has been considerable for some time is evident from a chapter titled "Shaping a New World Order" in *Imperial Brain Trust* (1977) by Laurence Shoup and William Minter, in which they printed a letter of resignation (unsent) dated September 14, 1942, from Harley Notter (assistant chief of the Division of Special Research, Department of State) that concerned

> relations with the Council on Foreign Relations. I have consistently opposed every move tending to give it increasing control of the research of this Division, and, though you [Pasvolsky, his superior] have also consistently stated that such a policy was far from your objectives, the actual facts already visibly show that Departmental control is fast losing ground.

Regarding the changing foreign policy agendas of the U.S. in the late 1980s, CFR chairman Peter G. Peterson said in the organization's 1989 annual report that "the Board of Directors and the staff of the Council have decided that this institution should play a leadership role in defining these new foreign policy agendas." Peterson has been chairman of Lehman Brothers, Kuhn, Loeb, Inc. CFR member Richard Holbrooke was managing director of Lehman Brothers before becoming assistant secretary of state under President Clinton and negotiating the Bosnian agreement. CFR member George Ball was chairman of Lehman Brothers in the 1960s after he was undersecretary of state. In 1993, CFR member Peterson wrote *Facing Up*, with an endorsement by Ross Perot on the book's jacket.

Early in January 1995, the *New York Times* Special Features sent over its wires an article by CFR president Leslie Gelb (a shortened version of his article in the CFR's November–December 1994 *Foreign Affairs*) in which he wrote: "The very long process of shaping a more effective and responsible United Nations must begin. This will require some sacrifices of sovereignty.... Multilateralism, ... is a fact not to be debated, but absorbed into American strategy." And in March 1995,

President Clinton nominated CFR member (and Trilateralist) John M. Deutch to be the new head of the CIA.

Remember that the ultimate goal of the New Age new world order promoters and planners is a socialist world government. And on C-SPAN, November 20, 1994, Milton Friedman, speaking on the fiftieth anniversary reissue of F. A. Hayek's 1944 book *The Road to Serfdom* (note the feudal "serfs" on the chart on page 127 of my book here will be you and me in the coming "techno-feudal socialistic New Age new world order"), said "It's a book well worth reading by anybody." Friedman explained that

> Socialism guides our behavior. . . . In practice, we keep moving down the Socialist road. . . . In fact, we are more than half Socialist today, that is, more than half the total output of the country is being distributed in a way that is determined by the government [including regulations]. . . . Bill Clinton is a Socialist, defined as somebody who believes that the way to achieve good things is to have government do it. You can't think of a more Socialist program than the health care program that he tried to get us to adopt.

Hayek warned that socialism was "the fatal conceit," which promised "equality" but resulted in equality of servitude to the state. Picking up on Hayek's reference to socialism as "the fatal conceit," Theodore Forstmann wrote about "the takeover of American life by government" in the *New York Times* (March 27, 1994, page F11) in the following terms:

> In the early 1900s, total spending at the Federal, state and local levels was 10 percent of the national income. By 1950, that figure had risen to 26 percent. Today, it stands at 43 percent and continues to grow. . . . For the first time, more Americans are employed by Government—18.7 million—than by manufacturing—18.1 million. . . . The United States, unfortunately, is moving toward democratic socialism. . . . And the Clinton Administration—which sees no task as too small, no dream too large, no issue too delicate for probing Government hands—has clearly joined the statist camp.

Friedman noted that Hayek's book was "dedicated to the Socialists of all Parties, and its thesis is that Socialism is paving the way toward totalitarianism."

In *The Decline of the West* (1926), Oswald Spengler noted that "ethical Socialism is *not* a system of compassion, humanity, peace and kindly care, but one of will-to-power."

The totalitarian Stalin in April 1924 said that according to Leninism, "a single world system of economy constitutes the material basis for the victory of socialism," and on May 18, 1925, he asked: "Did not Lenin say that there are two cultures—bourgeois culture and socialist culture—and that the demand for national culture is a reactionary demand of the bourgeoisie, which strives to infect the minds of the workers with the virus of nationalism?" (On September 29, 1988, Ted Koppel on ABC's "Nightline" also referred to nationalism as a "virus.") Then on June 27, 1930, Stalin further explained: "Lenin said that national oppression and national barriers will be abolished under socialism . . . [and] under socialism the interests of nationalities will become fused into a single whole" (the Marxian dialectic that Lenin called "disunion for the purpose of union."). This "fusing into a single whole" is happening with the European Community, as Flora Lewis in "The End of Sovereignty" (*New York Times,* May 23, 1992) wrote: "Some Europeans, like Margaret Thatcher, oppose letting European union nibble away at sovereign command within national borders because they consider Brussels [headquarters of the EC] likely to reintroduce socialistic tendencies."

To the left is the official stamp issued to commemorate the Second Election of the European Parliament, or the ECCCC (European Community Council for Cultural Cooperation). Note the similarity between the stamp and Revelation 17, which mentions a woman clothed round about, sitting on a beast on seven mountains and many waters, and an angel.

And another prominent member of the news media, Walter Cronkite, wrote in *A Reporter's Life* (1996): "If we are to avoid catastrophe, a system of world order—preferably a system of world government—is mandatory. The proud nations someday will . . . yield up their precious sovereignty." Cronkite would receive a World Federalist Association Global Governance Award, and in October 2005 he would write a letter stating: "As a long-standing supporter of Citizens for Global Solutions [formerly the World Federalist Association] and all it stands for, I encourage you to become a new member and register your support for an empowered United Nations."

Ross Smyth (Rotarian) in the November 1994 edition of *The Rotarian* wrote a letter "Towards Global Governance," in which he stated:

> Last fall, the Ninth World Citizens Assembly met in New York at the same time as the new Commission on Global Governance. The assembly participants, including myself, believe in the urgent need for democratic federal world government.... World law would apply directly to individuals, who would be charged effectively for major crimes against humanity. ... Because politicians will not yield power gracefully to allow the solution of major problems, the Commission on Global Governance realizes its principal challenge is to mobilize political will. It should clearly state its long-term objective of an *effective* system of world law.... Individual Rotarians should be more active in promoting the rule of law on a global basis. More than one million Rotarians can be at the vanguard as new world citizens who believe that the health of the human race takes priority over nationalism.

Luke 11:21 states that "when a strong man armed keepeth his palace, his goods are in peace." And Mark 3:27 says, "No man can enter a strong man's house, and spoil his goods, except he will first bind the strong man; and then he will spoil his house."

Sometimes the "binding" comes in the form of an appeal that socialism helps the poor more than capitalism does. However, when capitalist economic activities are used to promote biblical principles through charitable acts, capitalism is proven better than socialism even when it comes to helping the poor, as illustrated in the following example. A capitalist and a socialist each had $5,000 which they invested and doubled. The socialist gave all of his profit to the poor, but the capitalist kept $1,000 of his profit, giving only $4,000 to the poor. At first glance, it appears that socialism is more helpful to the poor than is capitalism. However, if the above process were repeated four more times, one would see that the socialist would have given $25,000 to the poor, but the capitalist would have given $30,000 to the poor while having $10,000 for himself (the second time, the capitalist would have invested his

$6,000, doubled that, given $5,000 to the poor, and kept $7,000, etc.).

During the years of the presidency of Bill Clinton the movement toward socialism came to be known as "the third way." And on January 8, 1999, President Clinton delivered a speech to the Detroit Economic Club in which he described what he believed "the role of government" should be in the following terms:

> Some have called this philosophy "the third way." It has modernized progressive political parties and brought them to power throughout the industrial world. Here in America it has led us, I believe, to a new consensus, making the vital center once again a source of energy, action and progress. That, I believe, is the only way for any advanced industrial nation to thrive in the new global economy.

In case you are in doubt as to whether "the third way" is socialistic, read what Rhodes Scholar E. J. Dionne, Jr., wrote in "A World Safe for Socialism" (*Washington Post*, April 27, 1999):

> The last thing the resolutely centrist and capitalist Democratic Leadership Council ever expected was a kind word to be said at one of its forums about—hold your breath!—socialism. But the DLC . . . found itself playing host Sunday (April 25) . . . to four Western European leaders whose parties have socialist and social democratic roots. . . . All subscribe to versions of the "Third Way" approach to politics that [Tony] Blair and Clinton have been marketing and that the DLC was celebrating. . . . [Italian prime minister Massimo] D'Alema said, "There are words that in your civilization, in your history, sound difficult to understand or to accept. For example, we belong to the *Socialist International,* and I'm aware that this word is somewhat sensitive here." . . . Still, the Third Way has largely been a successful defensive effort—it ended the Reagan–Thatcher era and gave liberals and, yes, socialists, presentable new clothes to wear.

For those who thought the movement toward socialism would be reversed with the election of George W. Bush as president in 2000, they were rudely awakened early in his administration by his (and Sen. Ted Kennedy's) "No Child Left Behind" legislation. It not only dramatically increased federal education spending, but also required all states to have their elementary and secondary education improvement plans approved by the U.S. secretary of education if they wanted to receive federal funding. So much for local control of education, as this movement toward more federal control is a movement toward socialism. For those who might say that this Bush education initiative does not mean an economic movement toward socialism in general, I would urge them to ponder the words of Andrew Card less than a year into the Bush presidency. On September 30, 2001, on "Fox News Sunday," Bush's chief-of-staff Card said he believed a combination of supply–side and Keynesian economics works best. John Maynard Keynes was the architect of modern British socialism. And if Hillary Clinton is elected president in 2008, the movement toward socialism in the areas of education, health, and the economy will rapidly increase.

However, if enough people become informed and politically engaged, the movement toward a world socialist government is stoppable. On May 7, 1995, Jacques Chirac, the conservative mayor of Paris (and former French prime minister) defeated the socialist candidate for the presidency of France, after the socialists had controlled that position for fourteen years.

The case for Christians becoming active in the formation of public policy can be found in "Taking a Stand: Why Christians Should Be Involved in Public Policy" (2006) by Stephen Danils, research director for the North Carolina Family Policy Council.

Hopefully, the American public will awaken soon and regain control of our republic from those who are moving us toward socialism and who threaten to diminish our heretofore constitutionally protected freedom and our nation's sovereignty by moving us toward a world government. Let us pray for God's help in our efforts.

Addendum

In *American Museum* (July 1792), Philip Freneau tried to warn the American people in what was then their young republic of what a power elite might try to do. His article, "Rules for Changing a Limited Republican Government into an Unlimited Hereditary One," was written from the perspective of the power elite (which Freneau opposed), and should be considered in terms of what has transpired in the U.S. between 1792 and today. Freneau said the power elite would emphasize the *limitations* of the republic's *Constitution,* with "precedents and phrases" (e.g., due process) "shuffled in." He next indicated that civil turbulence in the republic would be contrasted with the stability existing under the hereditary elite. The "grand nostrum" of Freneau's outline of the power elite's possible plan was the creation of *debt* "made as big as possible, as perpetual as possible, in as few hands as possible," and as complicated as possible. He then said, "A great debt will require great taxes. . . . Money will be put under the direction of government, and government under the direction of money" (e.g., banking elite). The next step would be to create "artificial divisions" within society (e.g., "divide and conquer" strategy) which would "smother the true and natural division between the few [elite] and the general mass of people, attached to their republican government and republican interests." Freneau then indicated that the elite would give a popular name, such as "the general welfare," to the usurped power so that those opposing the elite could negatively be labeled as "opposing the general welfare" of the people. He described how a military defeat (e.g., the Vietnam War) would be turned into political victory for the power elite. And lastly, he noted that those warning about the elite's attempt to seize power would themselves be labeled as "enemies to the established government." Freneau declared that this charge would "be reiterated and reverberated till at last such confusion and uncertainty be produced that the people, being not able to find out where the truth lies, withdraw their attention from the contest." This last element of Freneau's 1792 warning about a possible strategy of the power elite should be considered today particularly in terms of recent efforts to brand patriotic militia as right-wing extremists capable of violence.

Also of note, the "Father of Progressive Education" in the U.S., John Dewey, wrote a glowing article, "What Are the Russian Schools Doing?" in the December 5, 1928, edition of *The New Republic*. Read the following quotes from the article and see if any of them seem to relate to what is happening in American education today.

. . . the marvelous development of progressive educational ideas and practices under the fostering care of the Bolshevist government . . . the required collective and cooperative mentality. . . . The great task of the school is to counteract and transform those domestic and neighborhood tendencies . . . the influence of home and Church. . . . In order to accomplish this end, the teachers must in the first place know with great detail and accuracy just what the conditions are to which pupils are subject in the home, and thus be able to interpret the habits and acts of the pupil . . . as a skilled physician diagnoses in the light of their causes the diseased conditions with which he is dealing. . . . One of the most interesting pedagogical innovations . . . to discover the actual conditions that influence pupils in their out-of-school life : . . [is using] the themes of written work, the compositions of pupils, and also a detailed study throughout the year of home and family budgets. . . . This social behaviorism seems to me much more promising. . . . Thorough-going collectivists regard the traditional family as exclusive and isolating in effect and hence as hostile to a truly communal life. . . . The institution of the family is being sapped indirectly rather than by frontal attack. . . . There is no word one hears oftener than Gruppe, and all sorts of groups are instituted that militate against the primary social importance of the family unit. In consequence, to anyone who looks at the matter cold-bloodedly, free from sentimental associations clustering about the historic family institution, a most interesting sociological experimenta-tion is taking place. . . . Our special concern here is with the role of the schools in building up forces and factors whose natural effect is to undermine the importance and uniqueness of family life. . . . The earliest section of the school system, deal-ing with children from three to seven, aims to keep children under its charge six, eight, and ten hours per day, and in ultimate ideal this procedure is to be universal and compulsory. When it is carried out, the effect on family life is too evident to need to be dwelt upon.... [This is] part of a whole network of agencies by means of which the Soviet government is showing its special care for the laboring class ... and to give a working object-lesson in the value of a communistic scheme ... at deliberate social control.... Reference to this phase of Soviet education may perhaps be suitably concluded by a quotation from Lenin: "We must declare openly what is concealed, namely, the political function of the school.... It is to construct communist society."

The following five paragraphs were compiled by the United World Federalists, Washington, D.C., and printed in *Peace Through World Government* (1974) by George W. Blount.

Ex-president Harry S. Truman said, "When Kansas and Colorado have a quarrel over water in the Arkansas River they don't call out the National Guard in each state and go to war over it. They bring suit to the Supreme Court of the United States and abide by the decision. There is not a reason in the world why we cannot do that internationally."

Albert Einstein said, "Mankind's desire for peace can be realized only by the creation of a world government ... with all my heart I believe that the world's present system of sovereign nations can only lead to barbarism, war, and inhumanity, and that only law can assure progress toward a civilized peaceful humanity." Winston Churchill said, "The creation of an authoritative world order is the ultimate aim toward which we must strive." Jawaharlal Nehru said, "We have arrived at a stage where the next step must comprise a world and all its states, each having economic independence, but submitting to the authority of world organization." Charles de Gaulle said, "Nations must unite in a world government or perish."

Now at the beginning of the seventies, world events so emphasize the necessity and wisdom of world government to insure human survival as to make it indeed, "an idea whose time has come." The English historian Arnold Toynbee said in his book, *Experiences* (1969), "I believe that in the twenty-first century human life is going to be a unity again in all its aspects and activities. I believe that, in the field of religion, sectarianism is going to be subordinated to ecumenicalism; that in the field of politics, nationalism is going to be subordinated to world government; and that, in the field of human affairs, specialization is going to be subordinated to a comprehensive view" (*Experiences,* Arnold Toynbee, Oxford University Press, 1969, United States of America, p. 110).

The nations, once within the right direction, will increasingly lay their particular contribution upon the altar of humanity, and Tennyson's prophecy will come true:

> For I dipped into the future, far as human eye could see,
> Saw the vision of the World, and all the wonder that should be; . . .
> Till the war-drum throbbed no longer, and the battle flags were furled
> In the parliament of man in the Federation of the world. . . .
> There the common sense of most shall hold a fretful world in awe,
> And the kindly earth shall slumber lapt in universal law.
>
> —"Locksley Hall" by Lord Alfred Tennyson

(President Harry S. Truman carried in his pocket the part that predicted a "parliament of man, the federation of the world" explaining "that's what I have been working for.")

February 21, 1958   *CONGRESSIONAL RECORD-SENATE*   P. 2560

THE RELATIONSHIP BETWEEN FREE TRADE, FREE IMMIGRATION, AND WORLD GOVERNMENT

Mr. MALONE. Mr. President, a great editor, Mr. E. F. Tompkins, of the *New York Journal-American,* has written five important articles regarding the relationship between free trade, free immigration, and world government.

Mr. President, in a letter addressed to me, Mr. Tompkins stated:

"The free trade movement is not a separate entity. It is related in this country to the opposition to immigration regulations, and both by adoption or devolution are parts of the world government movement."

Mr. President, on Saturday, June 28, 1952, I said on the Senate floor—and my remarks were reprinted under the title "Free Economic System Versus Fabian Socialistic Program":

"Mr. President, the international socialism plan calls for—

(a) Reduction of all barriers to the flow of international trade.

(b) Access to raw materials of all sorts for all nations.

(c) Access to markets for all nations.

(d) A world organization through which the nations can share freely in the supplies and the markets of the world."

At that time, I also said:

"Mr. President, there can be only one result and only one final solution if these objectives are allowed to obtain, and that is, or course, the leveling of the living standards* of the United States of America with the sweatshop-labor nations of the world."

February 27, 1958   *CONGRESSIONAL RECORD-SENATE*   P. 3004-5

THE TRADE AGREEMENTS ACT

Mr. MALONE. Mr. President, I am happy that the American people could observe the coalition pushing the world distribution of American jobs and importing unemployment through free trade, or free imports.

The International Trade Organization, which was proposed when Mr. Acheson was Secretary of State, was part of the great plan to transfer distribution of American markets to Geneva. The ITO was rejected when it came before Congress, so the international free traders have brought forward the same scheme in the same package but under a different label.

Secretary Dulles, also a member of the great Hollywood extravaganza or the Washington circus to intimidate Congress, testified before the Senate Finance Committee in 1955, under my questioning, that:

---

* Congressman Peter DeFazio on May 3, 1995, will say this is also the result of NAFTA (see *Congressional Record,* May 3, 1995, p. H4533).

"The President may, at his discretion, sacrifice a part or all of any American industry, if he believes that his foreign policy would be furthered thereby."

This, Mr. President, is possible under the 1934 Trade Agreements Act as extended to June of this year.

Mr. President, in 1947, Mr. Truman, a part of this Washington circus of Tuesday, then President, transferred the constitutional responsibility of Congress to regulate foreign trade through the adjustment of the duties on tariffs to Geneva, Switzerland, under the operation called GATT, the General Agreement on Tariffs and Trade. All of this was done under the 1934 Trade Agreements Act, as extended.

Perhaps the most powerful element pushing for GATT has been the international banking community, which has been involved in our nation's history since its beginning. The most powerful banking family was the Rothschilds, and in *Twenty-Eight Years in Wall Street* (1888), Henry Clews (who twice declined the position of U.S. treasury secretary) wrote that M. A. Rothschild's "first great start in financial life was given to him by the use of the $20 million which was paid to Frederic II [a Mason] by George III of England for 17,000 Hessians to retain the American colonies."

Rothschild biographer Derek Wilson in *Rothschild: The Wealth and Power of a Dynasty* (1988) wrote that "constitutionalists resented it [the House of Rothschild] because its influence was exercised behind the scenes—secretly." And in Gustavus Myer's *History of the Great American Fortunes* (1936), one reads that "under the surface, the Rothschilds long had a powerful influence in dictating American financial laws. The law records show that they were the power in the old Bank of the United States." This bank, which existed from 1816 to 1836, was abolished by President Andrew Jackson, who warned: "The bold effort the present bank had made to control the government, the distress it had wantonly produced . . . are but premonitions of the fate that awaits the American people should they be deluded into a perpetuation of this institution or the establishment of another like it." The words, "the distress it has wantonly produced," referred to the statement by bank president Nicholas Biddle that "nothing but widespread suffering will produce any effect on Congress. . . . Our only safety is in pursuing a steady course of firm restriction [of money]—and I have no doubt that such a course will ultimately lead to restoration of the currency and the recharter of the Bank." Only a few years later, Karl Marx would have as Plank 5 of his *Communist Manifesto* that there should be "centralization of credit in the hands of the State, by means of a national bank with state capital and an exclusive monopoly."

Nathan Rothschild died the year President Jackson abolished the Bank of the United States, and eight years later, Benjamin Disraeli, (future prime minister of England) wrote *Coningsby* (1844) stating: "So you see, my dear Coningsby, that the world is governed by very different personages from what is imagined by those who are not behind the scenes." In this novel, Disraeli modeled the character Sidonia after Nathan Rothschild, saying that "he was lord and master of the money-markets of the world, and of course virtually lord and master of everything else." M. A. Rothschild supposedly once said, "Let me issue and control a nation's money, and I care not who writes its laws." And in Frederic Morton's *The Rothschilds* (1961), one reads that "someone once said that the wealth of Rothschild consists of the bankruptcy of nations."

At about the time Disraeli became prime minister, Cecil Rhodes began to develop his plan for world domination and become friends with Lord Rothschild. As Rhodes' biographer Sarah Millin wrote in *Rhodes* (1933): "Rhodes went to England to see Lord Rothschild, and Lord Rothschild approved of him." Rhodes (a Mason) also became friends with Winston Churchill, another friend of Lord Rothschild. Prior to the sinking of the *Lusitania,* Churchill had ordered a study of the political impact if Germany sank an ocean liner with Americans on board. And in *The Intimate Papers of Colonel House* (1926), one reads that on May 7, 1915, at 11:30 a.m., House met at Buckingham Palace with King George, who told him, "Suppose Germany should sink the *Lusitania* with American passengers on board." At 2:00 p.m., Germany sank the *Lusitania* (carrying munitions) with 128 American passengers! Colonel House was also the bankers' "inside" man in the Wilson administration helping to establish the Federal Reserve, which was part of a plan to bring about a type of new feudal order. And as an example of the socialist nature of this new feudal order of the future, one might remember the words of War Industries Board chairman Bernard Baruch on August 7, 1918 (printed in *The Knickerbocker Press* the next day in Albany, New York):

I should not hesitate to take anything anyone might have for his own advantage, if the taking would benefit the whole of society and help win the war. Every man's life is at the call of the nation and so must be every man's property. We are living today in a highly organized state of socialism. The state is all; the individual is of importance only as he contributes to the welfare of the state. His property is only as the state does not need it. He must hold his life and his possessions at the call of the state.

The House of Rothschild is generally associated with the Bank of England (for many years, the price of gold has been fixed each day in an upstairs room at N.M. Rothschild in London). The Bank of England got its start in the 1600s with funds from the Bank of Amsterdam (Netherlands) with the House of Orange (liberal Protestant-humanists), and the chairman and president of the Bank for International Settlements (central bank for all the world's central banks) from 1998 to 2003 was Willem Duisenberg (president of The Netherlands Bank). Other notes of interest concerning the Dutch are that Dutch funds supported Oliver Cromwell's revolution in England in the mid-1600s, and it was Dutch King William who became king of England in 1689 and established the Bank of England in 1694, following which debt to the bank quickly and greatly increased. The Rothschild and Warburg families have been close for centuries, and Max Warburg (who headed the German secret police during World War I) headed a banking group in Germany and Holland. Max's brother Paul was the architect of the Federal Reserve, which was supported during President Wilson's administration by Colonel House, whose family centuries before had come from Holland (George W. Bush also has some Dutch ancestors). Prince Bernhard of Holland would later form the Bilderbergers. And over the past several decades, Dutch groups have been quietly buying properties (e.g., shopping centers) in the U.S.

The Independent (April 3, 1902) published "The Next Step: A Benevolent Feudalism" by W. J. Ghent (former editor of *The American Fabian*) in which he wrote that the

coming status . . . will be something in the nature of a benevolent feudalism. . . . Group fidelity . . . is already observable. . . . The autocrats . . . will distribute benefits to the degree that makes a tolerant, if not satisfied people.... A person of offensive activity may be denied work in every feudal shop and on every feudal farm from one end of the country to the other.... His actions will be promptly communicated to the banded autocracy of dukes, earls and marquises of industries.... The individual security of place and livelihood of its members will then depend on the harmony of their utterances and acts with the wishes of the great nobles; and so long as they rightly fulfil their functions their recompense will be generous. They will be at once the assuagers of popular suspicion and discontent and the providers of moral and intellectual anodynes for the barons.... A host of economists, preachers and editors will be ready to show indisputably that the evolution taking place is for the best interests of all.... What the barons will most dread will be the collective assertion of the villeins at the polls; but this, from experience, they will know to be a thing of no immediate danger. By the putting forward of a hundred irrelevant issues they can hopelessly divide the voters at each election; or, that failing, there is always to be trusted as a last resort the cry of impending panic.... Two divisions of the courtier class are the judges and the politicians... They must satisfy the demands of the multitude, and yet, on the other hand, they must obey the commands from above.... The nobles will have attained to complete power, and the motive and operation of Government will have become simply the registering and administering of their collective will.... Armed force will, of course, be employed to overawe the discontented and to quiet unnecessary turbulence. Unlike the armed forces of the old feudalism, the nominal control will be that of the State.... When the new order is in full swing... so comprehensive and so exact will be the social and political control that it will be exercised in a constantly widening scope.... Peace (and stability) will be the main desideratum. ... A happy blending of generosity and firmness will characterize all dealings with open discontent.... [To] the prevention of discontent... the teachings of the schools and colleges, the sermons, the editorials... and even the plays at the theaters will be skilfuly and persuasively molded.

(Also see "The New World Order," by A. M. Rosenthal, *N.Y. Times*, May 5, 1998, p. A29.)

Ghent's book, *Our Benevolent Feudalism* (1902), was referred to in Jack London's *The Iron Heel* (1907) as "the textbook" the "oligarchs" would use to rule in the future. London said they (and the plutocrats) would have new ways "of moulding the thought processes of the nation," and that the banks would constitute

> one of the most important forces of the Oligarchy. . . . The labor castes, the Mercenaries, and the great hordes of secret agents and police . . . were all pledged to the Oligarchy. . . . The condition of the people of the abyss was pitiable. . . . All their old liberties were gone. They were labor-slaves. Choice of work was denied them. Likewise was denied them . . . the right to bear or possess arms. They were not land-serfs like the farmers. They were machine-serfs and labor-serfs.

Ghent wrote to H. G. Wells introducing "a lady who is very much interested in Socialism, who is going to England for more light. I suppose I have not impressed upon her sufficiently the heterodoxy of the Fabian School and you will thus probably find her an easy convert." Ghent signed the letter, "Your *revolutionary* comrade" (see copy of letter on next page). In H. G. Wells' *Anticipation of the Reaction of Mechanical and Scientific Progress Upon Human Life and Thought* (1901), mentioned earlier, he said that "the men of the new republic will have little pity and less benevolence. . . . [They] will not be squeamish either in facing or inflicting death. . . . They will have an ideal that will make killing worth the while. . . . The new republic will aim to establish . . . a world state with a common language and a common rule. All over the world its . . . control will run." Could the "comfortable merger" plan mentioned earlier by Ford Foundation president H. Rowan Gaither be that the former Soviet "republics" will be merged with our American republic to form "The New Republic" of H. G. Wells? Remember that Karl Marx said "democracy" was a necessary stage on the way to his final goal, and today one constantly hears the U.S. (incorrectly) referred to as a "democracy," which is what the former Soviet republics are also called. Perhaps the "comfortable merger" to "unite all democracies" is the interim stage before the final, all-inclusive, feudalist "New Republic" world socialist government.

Paving the way toward the power elite's global control are papers like "Global Interdependence and the Need for Social Stewardship" (1997) by the Rockefeller Brothers Fund as part of its "Global Interdependence Initiative" (on October 7–8, 1996, the Rockefeller Brothers Fund and the World Bank co-hosted a meeting entitled "Building a Constituency for Global Interdependence"). However, one should

Letter from *American Fabian* editor W. J. Ghent to H. G. Wells pay particular attention to an ominous characterization of what the future may be like under the control of a techno-feudal elite. This can be found in an "Opinion" column in the March 3, 1998, *Philadelphia Inquirer,* in which one reads: "If there is going to be a shortage of bright, well-educated people [in the future], corporations will pay a hugh premium to get them—even import them from overseas. They will then use these geniuses to design production systems that can be run by idiots, whom they will pay as little as possible to make up the difference." This sounds like the labor-serfs W. J. Ghent one hundred years ago predicted.

Because the largest threats to the new world order power elite are religious fundamentalists and patriotic nationalists, they will probably be labeled extremists, terrorists, or criminals, in an attempt to discredit them. Perhaps relevant to this is the fact that during the Oliver North hearings in Congress, Rep. Jack Brooks questioned North about his work for the National Security Council, saying "I read in several papers that there had been developed a contingency plan, in the event of an emergency, by that same agency [NSC] that would suspend the American Constitution." Sen. Daniel Inouye interrupted Representative Brooks, saying this was a "highly sensitive area" and requested "that that matter not be touched upon at this stage." Rep. Henry Gonzalez later commenting on this said "tragically Representative Brooks had been stopped by the chairman [Inouye]. The truth of the matter is that you do have those standby provisions, and the statutory emergency plans are there whereby you could, in the name of stopping terrorism, apprehend, invoke the military, and arrest Americans and hold them in detention camps."

That Representative Gonzalez mentioned "the military" and "detention camps" was interesting, because in 1994, C. Dean Rhody, director of Resource Management at Fort Monroe (Virginia) headquarters U.S. Army Training and Doctrine Command, sent a memo concerning "Draft Army Regulation on Civilian Inmate Program," stating that "the new regulation will provide the following: (a) Policy for civilian inmate utilization on installations, (b) Procedures for preparing requests to establish civilian inmate labor programs on installations, and (c) Procedures for preparing requests to establish civilian prison camps on installations." To verify this memo, I called Mr. Rhody's office on July 14, 1995, and aide Jean Nelson answered and referred to the memo as "the infamous letter." She said someone would get back to me about it, and a few minutes later, Fort Monroe public affairs officer Susan

Piedfort called me, saying the memo had been "leaked" by someone and therefore was "premature" because it was a "draft regulation" and "not final." Supposedly, these prison camps on military installations would just be used to house civilian inmates from states' overcrowded prisons, but it is still worth remembering Representative Gonzalez's statement.

Today's talk-show host Rush Limbaugh several times has ridiculed conspiracy theories, but on his February 7, 1995, national radio program, he remarked:

> You see, if you amount to anything in Washington these days, it is because you have been plucked or handpicked from an Ivy League school—Harvard, Yale, Kennedy School of Government—you've shown an aptitude to be a good Ivy League type, and so you're plucked so-to-speak, and you are assigned success. You are assigned a certain role in government somewhere, and then your success is monitored and tracked, and you go where the pluckers and the handpickers can put you.

And on his March 8, 1995, program, Limbaugh called the Clinton administration "socialist utopians." Interestingly, commentators have noted the similarity in policies between President Clinton and British prime minister Tony Blair, who has been a vice president of Socialist International (see president and list of vice presidents of this organization on page 129 of this book).

Conveniently, while media and press attention recently has focused upon *right-wing* militia as a threat to the U.S. government, little notice was given to the International Socialist Organization's (holding regular meetings at universities around the U.S.) promotion of "workers' militia" and its statement that "the struggle for socialism is part of a worldwide struggle.... To achieve socialism, the most militant workers must be organized into a revolutionary socialist party.... Only mass struggles of the workers themselves can destroy the capitalist system.... Capitalism must be overthrown ..." (*Socialist Worker,* November 22, 1996).

To show that the coming techno-feudal socialistic New Age new world order* was predicted many years ago, including free trade (today's World Trade Organization) as a vehicle toward it, note the following from the 1907 book, *Lord of the*

---

* See chart on page 117.

World, by Robert Hugh Benson (who wrote in it about "the Volor," a fast silent aircraft that could hover):

> ... in 1917 ... Communism really began. ... The new order began then. ... [After 1989] the final scheme of Western Free Trade. ... Esotericism is making enormous strides—and that means Pantheism. ... Humanitarianism is becoming an actual religion itself. It is Pantheism. ... Patriotism has been dying fast. ... [There is] this European parliament. ... [They believe] co-operation is the one hope of the world. ... [There will be] the alliance of Psychology and Materialism. ... With the Release Act in 1998 ... [there were] the ministers of euthanasia.* ... Julian Felsenburgh [Lord of the World] had a magnetic character ... rising out of the heaving dun-coloured waters of American Socialism like a vision. ... Felsenburgh's running the whole thing now. ... It will mean free trade all over the world. ... [His] speech consisted of a brief announcement of the great fact of Universal Brotherhood. ... The new era has begun. ... Party must unite with party, country with country, and continent with continent. ... Felsenburgh was called the Son of Man ... the Savior of the World. ... Persecution was coming. ... It involved all the stupendous force of Socialism directed by a brilliant individual. ... America was powerless: the balance of the world was overwhelmingly against her. ... This appearance of peace has deceived many. ... The press was engineered with extraordinary adroitness. ... The world is one now, not many. Individualism is dead. It died when Felsenburgh became President of the World. ... For any one to say that they believe in God—it is high treason. ... The Humanity Religion was the only one. Man was God. ... No actual point of light breaking the appalling vault of gloom. ...

---

*   In 1994, with passage of Measure 16, Oregon became the first U.S. jurisdiction to allow physicians to write prescriptions for terminally ill patients to use to commit suicide. In November 1994, Dr. Jack Kevorkian's lawyer said, "It's just the first domino to fall" (*New York Times,* November 11, 1994). Euthanasia supporters intend to promote similar suicide legislation in the states of Wisconsin, Florida, New Hampshire, Washington, California, and Texas. Over the past decade, as a result of various court decisions, both voluntary and involuntary euthanasia have become acceptable public policy in Holland, despite the fact that both practices are still technically illegal there.

Feudal Age*	Techno-Feudal Socialistic New Age New World Order
King	Big Brother
Princes and Princesses	International bankers
Knights of the Round Table	Cecil Rhodes' Round Table Initiates Helpers (Rhodes Scholars, CFR members, etc.)
Sheriff	U.N. Secretary-General (Head of U.N. Blue Helmet Army)
Dukes	Corporate heads
Lords and Overlords	World government leaders
Earls	Heads of nations (presidents, prime ministers, etc.)
Viscounts	Legislative leaders
Barons	Governors
Vassals (on fiefs)	Small businessmen (regulated by bureaucrats)
Serfs† and Peasants	You and me
Oafs (*originally, changelings or changeable persons*) and Knaves (*dishonest, deceitful persons; tricky*	Various political high officerholders; rascals; rogues
Human chattel	Human capital and human resources
Robin Hood and Men	Patriotic nationalists
Crusaders	New Agers promoting a "common faith" world religion (worshipping "Mother Gaia," etc.)
Abbots and Friars	Religious syncretists
Magicians and Wizards	World Health Organization (New Age esoteric alternative medicine)
Troubadours and Court Jesters	The media and the press
Dragon (fire-breathing)	The Beast (Revelation 13 and 17)

---

* Recent fashions (e.g., women's leotard-style pants), music (e.g., pan flutes), and hairstyles resemble those of feudal times.

† Many serfs paid a *smaller* percentage of what they produced than many people pay today in taxes.

"Beware of false prophets, which come to you in sheep's clothing, but inwardly they are ravening wolves"
—Matthew 7:15

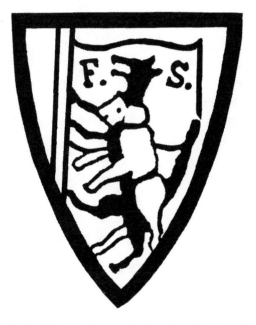

Coat of arms, showing the Fabian socialists' wolf in sheep's clothing, as depicted in *The Fabian Window* (1910) with H. G. Wells in the bottom left corner (see page 2). Almost a description of the 1990s, Wells in 1908 wrote in *First and Last Things:* "Socialism for me is a common step we are all taking in the great synthesis of human purpose.... [People] live in the mere opening phase of a synthesis of effort the end of which surpasses our imagination. Such intercourse and community as they have is only a dawn. We look towards the day, the day of the organized civilised world state. The first clear intimation of that conscious synthesis of human thought to which I look, the first edge of the dayspring has arisen—as Socialism, *as I conceive of Socialism*. Socialism is to me no more and no less than the awakening of a collective consciousness in humanity, a collective will and a collective mind."

Let us recall that the Socialist International in its present form, as its representatives tend to point out, was founded in 1951 at a congress in Frankfurt and that it considers itself a political descendant of the First and Second (Marxist) International.

XXI Congress of the Socialist International   1999

President:

Antonio Guterres

Vice Presidents:

Joaquín Almunia (PSOE, Spain)

Rolando Araya (PLN, Costa Rica)

Ehoud Barak (ILP, Israel)

Tony Blair (LP, Great Britain)

Leonel Brizola (PDT, Brazil)

Joaquim Chissano (Frelimo, Mozambique)

Hatuey de Camps (PRD, Dominican Republic)

Elio di Rupo (PS, Belgium)

Takado Doi (SDP, Japan)

François Hollande (PS, France)

Gyula Horn (MSzP, Hungary)

Erdal Inönü (CHP, Turkey)

Thorbjørn Jagland (DNA, Norway)

Ibrahim Boubacar Keita (ADEMA, Mali)

Viktor Klima (SPÖ, Austria)

Wim Kok (PvdA, Netherlands)

Paavo Lipponen (SDP, Finland)

Alexa McDonough (NDP, Canada)

Jaime Paz Zamora (MIR, Bolivia)

Göran Persson (SAP, Sweden)

Poul Nyrup Rasmussen (SDP, Denmark)

Gerhard Schröder (SPD, Germany)

Costas Simitis (Pasok, Greece)

Walter Veltroni (DS, Italy)

Abderrahman Youssoufi (USFP, Morocco)

Timoteo Zambrano (AD, Venezuela)

Index

About the Author

DENNIS LAURENCE CUDDY, historian and political analyst, received a Ph.D. from the University of North Carolina at Chapel Hill (major, American History; minor, Political Science). Dr. Cuddy has taught at the university level, has been a political and economic risk analyst for an international consulting firm, and has been a senior associate with the U.S. Department of Education. He has also testified before members of Congress on behalf of the U.S. Department of Justice. Dr. Cuddy has authored or edited twenty-two books and booklets, and has written hundreds of articles appearing in newspapers, including the *Washington Post, Los Angeles Times,* and *USA Today.* He has been a guest on numerous radio talk shows in various parts of the country, such as ABC Radio in New York City, and he has also been a guest on the national television programs "USA Today" and CBS's "Nightwatch."